W9-CAE-819

WITHDRAWN

77-577

TT
920
C7

Coyne,
The Penland School of Crafts
book of pottery.

Date Due

		JUL	2000
		JUN	2004
		JUL 09	
		JUL X X 2015	

THE PENLAND
SCHOOL OF CRAFTS
Book of
POTTERY

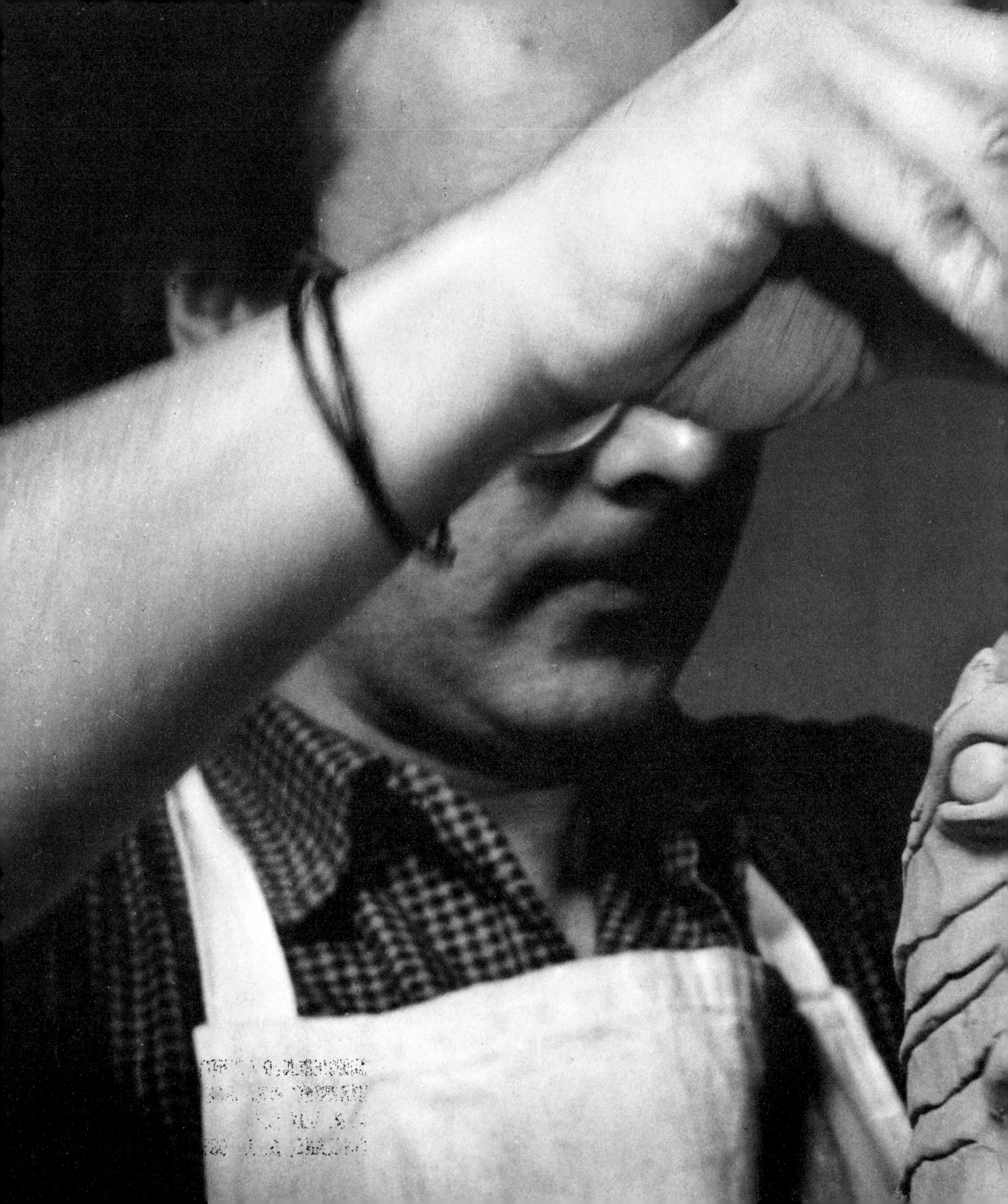

THE PENLAND SCHOOL OF CRAFTS

Book of POTTERY

Edited by John Coyne

with photography by Evon Streetman

A Rutledge Book
Bobbs-Merrill
Indianapolis/New York

Prepared and produced by Rutledge Books, 25 West 43
Street, New York, N.Y. 10036.

Published by The Bobbs-Merrill Company, Inc.,
Indianapolis/New York.
Printed in Italy by Mondadori, Verona. First printing.

Library of Congress Cataloging in Publication Data
Coyne, John.
  The Penland School of Crafts book of pottery.

  A Rutledge book.
  1. Pottery craft.   I.   Penland School of Handicrafts,
Penland, N.C.   II.   Title.
TT920.C7   738   74-34008
ISBN 0-672-51968-2

This book is dedicated to the artist-craftsmen who have come to Penland to teach. They have freely shared their knowledge and talents so that others might learn a craft.

For their advice and assistance we would like to thank Jane Brown, Bonnie Ford, John Ehle, Peggy and Charlie Dysarts, Jessie McKinney, Jon Ellenbogen, Betty Sue Hughes, Natalie Craig, Michael Robinson, Jane Hatcher, Jon Gray, Nancy Stanitz, Susan Silver, Frank Willis, Paul King, and Mary Cannon.

Contents

Editor's Note

Penland School has a very special place in the world of crafts. Year after year this school offers creative instruction in the major craft areas, taught by resident and visiting instructors who are among the finest in the world. Unfortunately, because of limited space, less than one thousand students each year are able to take advantage of Penland.

This space limitation was one reason why Bill Brown, Director of Penland, agreed to assist in the development of a series of books featuring the craftsmen of the school. He hopes that these books will be another way to share the talents of his unique faculty.

But Bill Brown and the craftsmen of Penland were not interested in doing just *how-to* books. They wanted a series that would accurately represent the school and also be a permanent example of the quality of instruction and the quality of creative work done here.

To achieve this, the instructors were asked to conceive of new pieces of pottery, construct these pieces, and, by using photographs and text, clearly explain the technical processes involved. All this work was done at Penland. Evon Streetman, resident photographer, took the photographs that accompany the text.

We believe that the pieces created by these ceramists are exciting and challenging enough to intrigue both potential craftsmen and experienced ceramists into trying out the projects themselves. At the very least, we hope the reader will learn much about the techniques and possibilities of pottery from this book.

Preface

Penland School of Crafts is a private, nonprofit organization in Penland, North Carolina, fifty-three miles northeast of Asheville and near the small town of Spruce Pine. It is the oldest, largest, and, we think, finest craft school in America.

Penland School was started by Miss Lucy Morgan in 1923. Miss Lucy once remarked to me that Penland was started "on a shoestring— and it frayed." Over the years it was built by Miss Lucy and others out of logs and bricks and glass and wallboard and pipe and nails and screws and other shoestrings, and keeping it all together has been a difficult task. But Penland was kept together, and it has grown. In 1923 Penland School was only one log building. Today we have thirty-three buildings on 380 acres of beautiful mountain land.

I have been at Penland School since 1962, and my wife and two boys and I have come to love it, and we have come to affectionately respect the people who travel to this high mountain community each year, where honest labor is particularly well favored. There is no finer community anywhere; there is no place where artistic, solid work is better appreciated, where artistic, solid people are more appreciated, or where I would rather work.

Thousands of people from North Carolina, from every state in the Union, and from over sixty foreign countries have come to this mountain community to learn to weave, to make pottery, and to work with wood, metal, glass, and stone. Some of these students have become professional craftsmen; many hundreds of others have developed an avocation that has been meaningful to them and their families.

We can now house, feed, and provide studio space for 130 people at each session. Last year we had over 700 students enrolled in our twelve courses. The only restriction we have is that a student must be at least eighteen years of age. We have college and art school students, grandmothers, doctors, lawyers, teachers (and they come in all colors)— anyone who wants to learn.

Students work an average of sixty hours per week in ceramics, weaving, glassblowing, graphics, photography, woodworking, vegetable dyeing, lapidary, plastics, jewelry, enameling, and sculpture. We have six sessions of two and three weeks during the summer and two special eight-week concentration courses in the spring and fall. For those who wish, both graduate and undergraduate college credit may be received for their work.

Throughout the year Penland sponsors a unique craftsmen's fellowship program for a limited number of well-trained craftsmen. These young people design, produce, and learn to market their work, using our facilities, for which they pay a nominal fee. Thus far we have helped ten craftsmen; they now own and operate their own studios and make a living producing their own work.

Penland has the finest faculty of any institution of its kind in the world. No other school could afford the salaries of the over seventy faculty members we have here during our sessions. We can't afford them either, so we don't pay them! They work for room and board, plus travel expenses. They do this because they believe that what we are doing here is worthwhile. These noted people donate the greatest gift we receive: their time, talent, and knowledge. They are the major reason for our success.

It is not our plan to increase the size of Penland, for it is felt that larger size would spoil the flavor of the school and destroy its educational quality. We must continue to grow in quality and to contribute in special ways to creativity in the crafts.

One way we hope to contribute is through a series of craft books. This particular book on pottery is one of the first in this series. Of the many fine ceramists who teach at Penland we have asked these artists to share their knowledge through instructional material and photographs.

As an educational institution, we think it is one of our responsibilities to make available the unique talents we have at Penland. If it is not possible for everyone to come and study here at our mountain school, we hope then that they can share, through these books, in the lives and skills of the talented people who have made Penland School of Crafts such an extraordinary place.

WILLIAM J. BROWN
Director

Formulas for Glazes

These are the most popular of the many glazes used at Penland School of Crafts. Many are named after the ceramists who first used them at the school.

Seacrest Purple
Cone 9–10 — Units

	Units
potash feldspar	537
whiting	129
colemanite	25
kaolin	60
flint	224
zinc oxide	25
	1000
3% black iron oxide	30
3% rutile	30

D-9 Yellow Brown
Cone 9–10

dolomite	313
whiting	40
potash feldspar	253
kaolin	323
flint	71
	1000
.5% cobalt carbonate	5
1% red iron oxide	10
2% bentonite	20

Iron Red Plum
Cone 9–10

Cornwall stone	422
dolomite	45
zinc oxide	10
whiting	112
kaolin	136
flint	275
	1000
2% bentonite	20
11.5% red iron oxide	115

Emily Purple
Cone 9–10

potash feldspar	410
colemanite	120
dolomite	70
talc	150
Tennessee ball clay	50
flint	200
	1000
2% bentonite	20
2% black cobalt oxide	20
2% tin oxide	20

Blue Green: Add — Units

	Units
5% cobalt carbonate	5
2% copper carbonate	20

Scripps Transparent
Cone 9–10

soda feldspar	462
whiting	174
zinc oxide	23
kaolin	109
flint	232
	1000

Alfred Yellow
Cone 9–10

dolomite	150
Cornwall stone	400
whiting	100
kaolin	250
flint	100
	1000
3% red iron oxide	30
5% rutile	50
2% bentonite	20

Temple White
Cone 9–10

potash feldspar	350
dolomite	197
whiting	26
kaolin	227
flint	200
	1000
2% bentonite	20

Temple Orange
Cone 9

Clinchfield (potash) feldspar	505
Cornwall stone	179
whiting	126
Tennessee ball clay	95
calcined kaolin	63
zinc oxide	32
	1000
2% bentonite	20
6% red iron oxide	60
4% rutile	40

Shaner's Red-Green
Cone 9–10

Kona A-3 spar (potash)	491
talc	40
kaolin	231
bone ash	38
whiting	200
	1000

Mamo White
Cone 9–10

potash feldspar	490
kaolin	200
whiting	40
dolomite	190
tin oxide	80
	1000
2% bentonite	20

Soft Albany (for salt)
Cone 9–10

Albany slip	416
wohastonite	167
calcined kaolin	417
	1000
2% rutile	20

Salt Slips
Cone 10

kaolin	157
ball clay	158
nepheline syenite	316
flint	316
borax	53
	1000

Colorants for above:

yellow pearly: rutile	15%
blue pearly: rutile	30%
cobalt	2%

Mather/Pitcher Salt Slips
Cone 9–10

feldspar	400
kaolin	400
lithium carbonate	100
borax	100
	1000
(a) cobalt carbonate	20
(b) red iron oxide	80
(c) rutile	80
(d) rutile	200

Spodumene
Cone 9–10

potash feldspar	283
spodumene	189
dolomite	212
kaolin	236
whiting	33
tin oxide	47
	1000
2% bentonite	20

4% red iron oxide	40
2% bentonite	20

Albany Slip
Cone 9–10

Albany slip	850
nepheline syenite	150
	1000
2% bentonite	20

Blue: Add

2% cobalt carbonate	20

Toshiko Semi-Matte White
Cone 9–10

Kona F-4 spar	374
kaolin	187
Cornwall stone	187
whiting	187
zinc oxide	65
	1000
2% bentonite	20

Semi-Matte Black
Cone 9–10

Toshiko Semi-Matte White base (above)	1000
20% red iron oxide	200
5% cobalt carbonate	50
1% manganese carbonate	10

Ann's Blue
Cone 9–10

potash feldspar	896
whiting	104
	1000
3% rutile	30
2% red iron oxide	20

Ocher Celadon
Cone 9–10

ball clay	136
whiting	182
flint	272
potash feldspar	365
dolomite	45
	1000
2% yellow ocher	40

Celadon
Cone 9–10

flint	324
whiting	198
potash feldspar	275
kaolin	203
	1000
2.5% red iron oxide	25

Sources of Supplies

Clay

Ron Propst
Box 29
Penland, North Carolina 28765

Leslie Ceramic Supply Company
1212 San Pablo Avenue
Berkeley, California 94706

Standard Ceramic Supply Company
P.O. Box 4435
Pittsburgh, Pennsylvania 15205

Rovin Ceramic Supplies
6912 Schaefer Road
Dearborn, Michigan 48126

Van Howe Ceramic Supply Company
11975 East 40th
Denver, Colorado 80239

Magazines

Craft Horizons
44 West 53 Street
New York, N.Y. 10019

Ceramics Monthly
Professional Publications Inc.
1609 Northwest Boulevard
Columbus, Ohio 43212

Lusters

Nils Cederborg Associates
Renaissance Lusters
P.O. Box 20093
Columbus, Ohio 43221

Handbook for Users of Liquid Bright Gold
Made by Hanovia Liquid Gold of
Engelhard Industries
East Newark, New Jersey 07029

Decals

Cerami Corner Inc.
607 North San Gabriel Avenue
P.O. Box 615
Azusa, California 91702

Glaze Materials

Rovin Ceramic Supplies
6912 Schaefer Road
Dearborn, Michigan 48126

Building by Hand and Heart
Paulus Berensohn

Paulus Berensohn has been associated with the Penland School of Crafts for seven years as instructor and resident fellow, and makes frequent trips there as a visiting scholar. While in residence at Penland he wrote the book Finding One's Way With Clay. *Currently he leads workshops around the country and is working on two new books.*

In a workshop that I led recently, a young sculpture student made a remark that I found very interesting.

"You know," she said, "clay is the only material that my sculpture teacher does not allow us to use."

"Why?" I asked.

"He says clay is too responsive, that it never stops."

Somehow, instead of hearing this statement as she repeated it, I kept hearing "clay never stops" over and over in my head like the ringing of a bell. I repeated it out loud.

"How extraordinary. Clay never stops!"

It seemed a very real and dimensional description, no longer a negative one. As I said it, an image appeared in my head of a tabletop covered with clay. Every day I would work on and change the form of the clay, adding and deleting; it would be a piece that would never end, never stop, as long as I was able or needed to continue.

I do suppose that clay has its limitations; certainly different clays have their own individual characteristics. But I do not think that any of us yet knows—or will ever know—all the possible shapes that clay can take. Clay seems to take all we may need to give it.

One of the limitations some of us may feel is the limitation of skill. We do not yet have the power in ourselves to make a real and alive connection with our clay, so that what we need to do we are *able* to do. We feel that this limitation may lie in actually handling the clay. Hand building with clay is no less technically challenging and mystifying than making pots on the potter's wheel. But whereas the wheel requires a serious discipline—in a specific and historic way—that calls for repeated practice and fidelity, like playing the piano, in hand building we may use several methods, traditional or contemporary, depending upon what we want to do. Each of us, building on what we are offered by our teachers, finds our own touch—for no one teacher can possibly show us all the ways to hand build. Each method requires both an individual relationship and individual practice—not only in choices between pinching, coiling, and working with slabs of clay, but in the actual way we pinch, coil, and slab. Whether we blend the coils into each other architecturally or let

14

them stand visible, use a fine coil or a massive one, a flat or a rounded, rolled or squeezed, textured or smoothed into a long and continuous plastic line—all are choices only we can make.

In this volume we witness nine experienced and skillful artists—hand builders and wheel potters—speaking their own individual languages with clay. These are artists of considerable maturity; we join them, here, at a point where many troublesome problems have been solved. We see each of them working, step by step, on one individual piece; at the same time we are able to read valuable discussions about how they are doing it and why they may be doing it in just this way. It represents a kind of method-sharing one is not accustomed to finding except in personal one-to-one conversation.

Yet I do not wish to characterize the bodies of work included in this volume solely as works of skill in handling materials. It is their individual expressiveness that I find inspiring and helpful. What compels me most about their work is how different each artist is from the other—not just in the way each works, but in personality and lifestyle. To me, the people who made these pieces are the *why* of what we feel and experience when we look at their work with openness and receptivity. For, in fact, each has a point of view and an individual connection to his or her imaginative life. The artists are not merely constructing pots and sculpture, but working with images, gestures; they are being expressive.

It is possible to be expressive with clay from the very first day one hand builds with it, even while working out the problems and practicing for strength. It requires no less skill and probably much more to be expressive, to be open to images and to carry them through. One can learn to play the piano, but to play Chopin with feeling requires more. We can learn how to put coils together, but how do we make them sing? These are important questions. How do we go about developing more and increasingly deeper skills of expression and imagination? To build by hand with clay we have to, and can, strengthen and develop the muscles of the heart and the inner eye at the same time we increase our abilities to handle and listen to our clay.

There have been step-by-step books before, as well as volumes illustrating a select group of artists. Combining these two approaches, as this book does, and on the level of craftsmanship offered, is an important and useful step forward. Both the student and the teacher in me are thankful. The teacher is supported in his belief that he can offer what he feels alive in him and guide his students to others, to a book such as this one, in an area where he feels his interest and experience are less evolved. The student is given an opportunity for learning that goes far beyond his normal enthusiasm for it, because he encounters actual works.

Yet the contemporary artist-craftsman and student is faced, now, in the last quarter of the twentieth century, with what might be called an embarrassment of riches. Fifty years ago or less, we might have been aware of the work of other craftsmen, if they lived nearby; and through books and museums, if we were fortunate enough to have them available, we might have had an historical contact—but generally, we had little choice of whom to study with or apprentice to, and we were largely unaware of technical and artistic developments that might be taking place only a few miles away. Today, through our mobility, the proliferation of galleries exhibiting craft work, the enormous increase of courses, workshops, and demonstrations, and several very available periodicals, we are all well aware, if we choose to be, of work being created all over the world.

While we may welcome this, there is also the danger that we may be only superficially aware of what's going on. Our heads can get too full of other peoples' abilities and other peoples' images. How do we find our own way? All that information can be overwhelming, unless we make real use of it to help evolve our *own* connection to the materials we work with and to the development of our own language of expression. This book is made for *use* in one's head, hands, and spirit, and there are undoubtedly many ways to make use of it. I would like to suggest here, briefly, two ways: copying and imitating.

Many of us have negative associations with the words "copying" and "imitating." We may feel uncomfortable when our work resembles the work of others, and perhaps even angry when we believe that our work has been "lifted," "ripped off," or duplicated. We may certainly feel this way with reason when we see the work in exhibitions. I do not mean to suggest copying and imitating here as a way of doing our work. I offer it as a discipline of *learning* our work, our material.

For me, to copy is to duplicate. Now one can duplicate a pot from the way it looks by adopting the pallet of clay and glazes, the methods of firing, the appearance of the form; but we may then, and usually do, miss the real opportunity. If we can duplicate as a meditative discipline, if we can be in dialogue in our imaginations with the original maker of the piece, we may begin to connect to a new skill, a fresh insight, and a real understanding of a form—from the inside. We put the piece before us and ask questions. Why is the handle that size? What if I made it larger and put it here? By putting it here I've changed the whole feeling of the form. How does it look and feel here as opposed to the way it looks there? We ask these questions as we work, not so much in a search for answers but more in the hope of coming to a feeling of why the artist may have made the decisions, performed the acts he or she did. In this way we reproduce a form in order to have an experience of it; in experiencing the form, it may then become a possible choice of one's own. Duplicating the work of others can be a way of enriching one's feeling for form, of developing a more informed forming eye and hand. The point is not to make a perfect duplication; the point is to learn to ask the right questions, to come to a feeling, an intuition, and to have the experience of how another works in order to lay a more fertile ground on which to build an individual way of working. To find out for oneself, with the piece as teacher guide, is the ideal way.

The dictionary defines "imitate" as "to copy the appearance, the mannerisms of: to reproduce." This is not what we are after if we are truly committed students of the evolving artist in ourselves and others. I think it is helpful to make a distinction between copying (duplicating) and imitating, and to see imitating as *carrying an image on.* In this way we can look at work and, as students, practice the dynamics of imagination. In Bruno LaVerdiere's "Arch" I may see "doorway." Doorway into what? From where? By carrying his image on through me, I may be inspired to make a series of miniature archways that are thresholds into new lands I feel I would like to explore. Or I might place myself in the "tension of the arch," going in and coming out. It is possible to practice imaginative skills in this way, if we carry the images we behold and have a feel for into us and let them change as we observe and listen.

Most of us are untrained in imaginative skills; imagination is, in fact, rarely taught. One first step we can take for ourselves is to look at the images in work that compels us and leads us to nonanalytical deep listening. Not passive admiration, but the active bearing of an image or idea, carrying it on into us and out through our hands into our clay. It's an important practice.

In this book, Penland School of Crafts offers to others that special quality of mixed pollinization and support that one receives when one is fortunate enough to be at the school as student, instructor, or resident fellow. In the seven years I have been associated with Penland, almost fifty different potters have taught or conducted workshops or given demonstrations, for periods ranging from two days to eight weeks, most of them returning again and again. No one point of view about clay, but a life with clay, or what can or should be made with clay, is fostered. Penland has no ax to grind. It is a dynamic community, always changing, allowing and seeking out alternative voices, always supporting and celebrating. I think of Penland as a place in which people take an interest in one another and learn from each other as students, teachers, friends, and associates. It is up to us to carry on this relationship, to receive the greeting, to take the hand and build with it and from it with feeling.

On Throwing
Robert Turner

Robert Turner, professor of sculpture and pottery at Alfred University, is a leading authority on the art of throwing. He first came to Penland as a student in the late 1930s, while still an undergraduate at Black Mountain College in North Carolina. He has taught at Penland and has given workshops and lectures at leading ceramics schools throughout the country.

What shall I throw?" Don asked.

"Throw a typewriter," called Pete.

Instead Don threw a superb large pitcher. In any case, as we all know, you don't throw typewriters, you hand build them. As for throwing, the word "turning" may have a safer ring, but "throwing" is more apt—to the dynamism of the process, and to the potter's belief that a pot should conform to "the inner principles of growth"—without denying that the throwing wheel can be used for many aims.

Throwing is a fantastic, life-exploding process. It seems to transform and to raise the level of the energy brought to it, almost a quantum jump. Clay plunked on a senseless, spinning wheel cannot of itself create energy—you must always bring *your* energy to the process. Many a dull pot attests to this obvious but crucial point. The ability to throw is not the source of the life of a pot: anyone can learn to throw, even a machine.

The great potters that we can think of worked with love, vigor, and sensitivity. They transmitted their strength. Such work has an intensity of being: it is, it acts.

The sense of being in the thrown pot—the sense of "life"—is based upon events intrinsic to the throwing process—that is, the unexpected and the transforming. Thus, perhaps most among all art media, the act of making by throwing is life giving, from the transforming action upon all elements of the process—idea, clay, and potter. The potter as well as the clay is altered.

18

A warning here: as a mesmerizing activity, throwing can become self-serving if entered by potters without enough idea of what they are about. The wheel *is* captivating! In society, the skill of performing can be spellbinding.

Great pots, however, show not only mastery of skills but also purposeful use of tools. Toshiko Takaezu, Donald Reitz, Cynthia Bringle, and Ron Propst use the wheel knowingly, as a tool, however magical. It is their sense of purpose that is central.

The great pottery of the Han culture—like the rugged early American salt-glaze pickle jars made for back-country storage—shows the strength of purpose and of idea. And I conclude that this underlying strength, the possession of a personal and cultural base, gave particular direction to the energies of the masterful potters who made those pieces. The utilitarian, or pop, or image-idea juxtapositions of today are simply directions, categories, ways of putting the material together. Neither good nor bad in themselves, they are irrelevant to what greatness, or even conviction, is about. An object becomes convincing only through the conviction of the person who made it. A convincing pot results only if the potter knows, by a root he has or is developing, why he is making it.

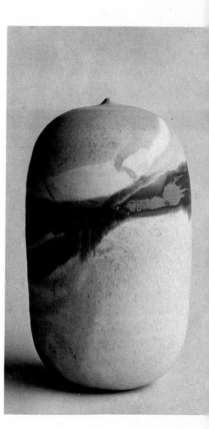

Perhaps identity is the word we need here. We have lost the sense of identity that the village potter or wood carver had whose work and whose village were interdependent in the continuity of life itself. We have no cultural imperative in that powerful sense. And where do we find personal identity? We must develop our own, from whatever inner sense or flicker of light we may have.

People use the wheel and clay in changing ways as needs change. Unlike the traditional European craftsman who follows given specifications, the artist senses needs, both personal and cultural.

Historically, pottery has always been made both for use and for ritual (identity), in varying proportions depending upon the needs of the culture. Producing in quantity commences as people begin to specialize. The emphasis upon utility then grows, and with cities as the market, the loss of a belief common to all decreases the ritual basis of many pieces.

The person whose identity both grows with and communicates through his pottery provides a sense of identity for others, too. The thrown pot still provides a unique opportunity for such communication.

Given the opportunity to form with the hands, people express the common need for both physical and spiritual life; the vital may be found. In the tension of dance is the tension of the pot; the rhythms of the pot are the elements of song.

Tyrone: I never had any formal training in pottery; I started using slabs because it was a way of becoming involved with clay without having the technical skills to throw properly. My first exposure to ceramics was through Julie, who had studied art at the State University of New York at Buffalo and with William Pitney at Wayne State University, where she obtained her Master's degree in pottery. My education and work experience were in a totally different area. I worked for the United States Corps of Engineers as a Navigational Cartographer in the Lake Survey Division. My section surveyed and drew up navigation charts of the Great Lakes. It was while charting Lake Ontario and working near Oswego, New York, that I first met Julie.

In 1966, when Julie completed her Master's degree, I resigned from the Corps of Engineers and we opened a studio/shop in Royal Oak, Michigan. We were greatly influenced by John Glick, a potter in the Detroit area, who a few years before us had begun to work full-time as a production potter. John showed us—and a good many other potters—that it was possible to make a living from pottery. At the time few people were doing production pottery on a full-time basis. John has continued to be a close friend and an inspiration to us both.

Julie and I have been making our living as production potters since 1966. The two hexagons we construct here do not come under the heading of production pieces. Many of the pieces pictured in this book are not production items, but rather the personal statements we make in clay, which act as a balancing point for our production work. When Julie and I find ourselves tiring of bowls, boxes, jars, and planters, we usually stop and do a piece such as these lustered hexagons. Although we combine much lustering and slab building in our production work, the pieces are not of this scale. Then, after a piece or two of the complexity of these—especially Julie's—we are both ready to go back to the simpler designs we have developed, and the cycle begins again.

Potters' lives seem to flow in cycles. The main cycle, of course, centers around the firing of the kiln. The pots are made, must dry, are bisque-fired, then glazed and fired again. Our cycle is extended to include two luster firings after the final stoneware firing. As we do much of our own selling at art fairs, a fair usually means the end of a cycle; if not a fair, we would be delivering pots to fill a wholesale order. And a trip is involved in almost every cycle.

A normal working cycle for us usually consists of two or three stoneware firings in our gas kiln, which holds approximately 125 pieces per firing. Our cycles average about six to eight weeks in length. Un-

Figure 1. The slabs are cut by drawing wire through the block of clay.

Figure 2. Hexagon slabs are cut to size with templates.

fortunately art fairs don't always schedule themselves to fit our cycles of work, so to accommodate them we must sometimes compress everything into less time. Life becomes quite hectic at those times, and when the weatherman doesn't cooperate, things really get tight. When it rains for a week, as it sometimes does in the mountains, pots won't dry and consequently can't be bisque-fired on schedule. Somehow things work out, though, for we've never missed a fair we were scheduled to attend.

While we were living in the Detroit area most of the fairs we attended were within a one-day drive from home. Though this made fair-going easier, we found the city environment not to our liking. Our busy showroom, which had sustained us in the beginning and helped us to build a following, became more and more of a drain on our time. We spent a great deal of time waiting on customers and chatting with friends who dropped by. After five years in Royal Oak we decided it was time for a change. Jane and Mark Peiser, resident craftsmen at Penland, suggested North Carolina, so we visited them in 1971. Now we're in the mountains for good; they offer us all the peace and serenity we had been looking for. Our lives are still very hectic at times; the working cycles haven't changed that much, and the trips to art fairs now take two days instead of one. But when it all starts to catch up with us we can climb the hill that's behind our house, and just sit and relax and just count the mountain ranges.

Country life seems natural to both our characters. Julie grew up on a farm and though I was born and raised in Detroit, I adjusted immediately. Our lives have taken on new aspects since our move. In addition to making pottery, we have acquired an interest in gardening, and we now raise most of our own vegetables. We have planted an orchard and are considering raising chickens and other small farm animals. We would like to see all our activities become part of an integrated lifestyle, with each segment balanced and natural. We have a long way to go, but we seem to be moving toward that goal.

We now live in a small community comprised of warm and friendly people. Much of the land in our valley is dairy-farmed by Guy Silver, who can trace his ancestors back seven generations to the very people who settled Bandana and the surrounding mountain areas. Those early ancestors were given this wilderness land as veterans' benefits for serving in the Revolutionary War with George Washington. A commemorative marker still stands in the tiny cemetery at Kona. Our neighbors love the land and enjoy a peaceful and settled way of life. And we are learning much about living from them.

Figure 3. Edges of slabs are miter-cut to a 30-degree angle on back side of slabs.

Figure 4. Edges of slabs are all scored.

When we first moved here we were afraid we might be considered outsiders. But this never happened. We were readily accepted as part of the community, though it was partially due—in the beginning—to the fact that we were working with our hands. Because many of our neighbors work in craft-related industries, such as the furniture and textile industries, they can appreciate our involvement with a craft. We also use the raw materials mined in this area, such as the feldspars, flints, and kaolins. And many of the men have, at one time or another, worked in these mines; they are an important part of the economic picture of this area. So they can relate to our pottery, too, through the materials which go into its composition. As friends, they become involved in what we are doing in pottery in much the same way as we become involved in their farming activities. And though our activities vary, we can always agree on one thing—the weather. As Guy jokingly commented at the milking barn one dreary day, "Wet weather is bad for hay and clay." After the anonymity of city life, we find our lives have been greatly expanded by these warm and friendly relationships we have developed in this community.

My approach to ceramics hasn't changed much over the years. I like hand building and I particularly like working with the slab technique. I also like to work precisely, as one would suspect from my training as a cartographer.

Though clay is not very accurate by nature, I push it as accurately as I can in hand building. I could use molds, but then I would be deprived of the assembling part of the process and the hand-built quality would be lost, as would the integrity of each individual piece. I enjoy the planning involved so that all parts will fit together when they're assembled. Many potters find it difficult to work with slabs as there are so many processes that aren't creative, such as cutting the slabs and setting them to dry. I don't mind that type of preparation, and I get very excited when I actually assemble the pieces and create the finished form.

I do pots in families. The size of the piece determines how many I will make at one time. I usually make small cubes and boxes in groups of eight or ten. When I do canister sets in four graduated sizes, I do four or five of each size at a time.

For the pots we make here I'll make enough slabs for two hexagons, one of which I will decorate with decals and lusters. The second hexagon Julie will carry a step further in construction and decorate with a coil design applied to the surface. In doing that, she will completely

Figure 5. Slurry is applied to scored edges.

alter the finished piece and come up with a totally different statement. Both pots, though they begin the same, end up very different from each other, as complete and distinct entities.

The clay formula we use for all our stoneware work is designed to use readily available materials and meet all our needs as a general all-purpose clay body. The A.P. Green fireclay and the Cedar Heights clay give the body strength to stand Cone 10 firing—2350° F. The ball clay improves the plasticity for throwing on the wheel, and the grog is just coarse enough to "open the body" in order to avoid the warping and cracking problems in drying slab-built pieces.

Our formula:

A. P. Green fireclay	100 pounds
Cedar Heights Gold Art clay	150 pounds

Kentucky ball clay O.M. #4	25 pounds	
potash feldspar	12 pounds	
flint	6 pounds	
20/28 mesh grog	20 pounds	

Figure 6. Sides are joined to the base of the hexagon.

We mix our clay several thousand pounds at a time in a pug mill, a special machine that mixes the clay in an auger and extrudes it in a four-inch-diameter tube. We store the clay in plastic bags.

For these two hexagons I've wedged two lumps of clay of twenty pounds each. The wedging removes any air pockets and evens the consistency. One lump is roughly formed into a rectangular block, the other into a round form. I cut the clay slabs with a system of blocks of hardwood into which nails have been set at even intervals. The spaces between the nails correspond to the thickness of the slabs. A wire with loops at each end is hooked over the nails and drawn through the block of clay. (Figure 1) By raising the wire up one nail per slice, I soon have the twenty-pound block sliced into seven or eight slabs of clay. The round will make four or five slices.

I cut the pieces from the block instead of rolling them because I've found that rolling stretches the particles of clay, causing the slabs to warp in the drying. By using the block process, I eliminate much of that warping. The slices are next peeled off and spread out on my table.

When working with slabs of this size, a good deal of drying space is necessary. I work on a table that is covered with a four-by-eight-foot sheet of plywood. This plywood has been marine-varnished so that it is waterproof. Over this plywood I have stretched a heavy canvas. This is all necessary because when I set the wet slabs down to be assembled, I can work on them without the fear that they will stick to the surface of the plywood. The canvas also absorbs moisture, assisting in the drying.

I let the rough slabs dry on the table until leather hard. This means they are still moist but have lost enough moisture so that the slab will hold its shape when stood on end. This you learn by practice, for the time involved in bringing the slabs to the leather-hard state depends on the thickness of the slab and the weather. I am using rather thick slabs ($3/8$ inch) for these large hexagons, so it will probably take ten to twelve hours for them to dry to leather hard. It's best to keep a close watch on them, as the time always varies.

During the drying stage, while the slabs are spread out on the table, I use the edge of a piece of Plexiglas to smooth over the rough grog tracks, which were pulled up by the wire during slicing. This leaves the surface free of grog holes, which tend to cause pinholes in the glazed piece.

An important point to remember in slab construction is that all the slabs must be of the same consistency—moisture-wise—or they will not hold together properly. If I find the slabs are not drying evenly, or if I can't work on them when they reach the leather-hard stage, I restack them on a sheet of thin plastic and wrap them securely with the plastic sheeting to stand overnight. In a few hours the moisture content will be evened out. I then spread them back out on the table for cutting.

Cutting the slabs into proper shape is done with a plastic template and a potter's knife. I have templates of various sizes and shapes, and for this hexagon I use a template that is six inches wide and twelve

Figure 7. Excess slurry is pressed out by applying pressure to the edges.

inches long. I expect to get about 12 percent shrinkage from wet clay to finished piece, so I take that into account when deciding on what size I want the pot to be in its final form. I cut three rectangular slabs, trim them to size, then cut them in half. This gives me the six sides I need for my hexagon. (Figure 2) This particular hexagon has sides that are six inches high, but that could be varied. The sides might be as high as eight inches on a tall pot or as low as two inches. I next take another template, shaped in the form of a hexagon, and cut out two hexagonal slabs from the round slices. These slabs will form the bottom and the top of the pot. I repeat the same cutting process and I have enough slabs for two hexagons.

Figure 8. Coil is added to the inside of the seam to aid in holding the slabs together.

The slabs at this point still have square corners, so to ensure that they will fit together properly, I miter-cut the edges just as if I were working with wood. (Figure 3) The angle that I cut is at 30°—there are six sides and there are 60° in each angle, which makes 360° in the circumference. If I were making a box, I'd have the angles at 45°. This, of course, is not a perfect 30° angle, but in assembling I can force the correct shape. One thing to remember here: All the square slabs must be turned over before the miter is cut or the side you have smoothed will be on the wrong side of the pot—the inside! I guess you could smooth both sides to avoid forgetting, but I never do—though I also forget occasionally.

Figure 9. With a wooden tool, the coil is smoothed down into the corners.

Figure 10. Calipers are used to measure the inside of the flange.

Before joining any two pieces together, I first score the clay. (Figure 4) Scoring and the use of slurry (a thin mixture of water and the clay body that is being used) is necessary when joining two pieces of clay together that are leather hard. It creates a strong bond between the pieces of clay, much as if they had been glued together. I score both pieces of clay with a sharply pointed instrument, such as a fork, then brush in slurry. (Figure 5) The slurry makes the seams wet and fills in the clay where it has been scored. Once all the slabs are scored and slurried I begin constructing by attaching the sides to the bottom slab. (Figure 6) The pieces of clay are then hand-pressured together, and all the excess slurry is pressed out. (Figure 7)

When all the sides are attached, I next place thin coiling around the inside of the seams. (Figure 8) The coils help hold the slabs together,

Figure 11. Again, calipers are used to measure the lid flange.

for joined slabs have a tendency to come apart when drying. But if the coils are too thick, they can trap air inside the seams and cause more problems than they prevent. I therefore use very thin coils and smooth them down in the joints so that it looks as if the corners and edges have been rounded slightly. To do this I use a simple wooden tool that is rounded at the end, running the tool along the edges. (Figure 9) While using the tool, I hold my fingers on the outside of the slab to make sure I don't push out the newly formed seam. I now have the six sides in place and joined to the base hexagon.

I now need to construct the foot, flange, lid, and knob, and for this I go to the potter's wheel and throw the basic forms.

The foot is thrown first, using the measurements I've worked out on the hexagon template. As I throw, I check the size with calipers

Figure 12. The knob is thrown and added to the lid.

to make sure the dimensions are correct. Accuracy is important because I want the top of the foot to be at the edge of the hexagon slab. And the foot must support the weight of the pot during the drying. The foot should be thrown to the approximate thickness of the slabs, though I give the bottom a thicker bead to lend physical and visual strength to the form.

The flange (or ring) for the top must also be thrown with great care. I measure the hexagon template with a caliper and throw a flange so that the inside edge measures $8^5/8$ inches. (Figure 10) The flange is thrown with a thick wall, leaving a bead of clay at the top where the lid will set.

The final throwing process is the lid, which is done much like throwing a bowl. Measurement here is critical because the inside lip of the lid must fit down into the flange with some clearance but not too much play. Lid measuring is another technique developed only by constant practice. (Figure 11)

When the lid reaches a leather-hard stage it is removed from its plaster bat, turned over and recentered on the wheel, and trimmed to form a smooth curve. A small lump of clay is attached to the center of the lid with scoring and slurry, then the knob is thrown to the desired shape. (Figure 12) When these parts are thrown they must be allowed to stiffen to the same consistency as the slab walls, a process that again takes time. I sometimes throw the parts before I construct the slabs so they can be drying while I'm working on the hexagon.

To set the foot and top ring on their slab hexagons, I work at a treadle kickwheel. I use this wheel because it is easier to control the position of the piece while working. I center the remaining hexagon slab on the wheel head. I then center the top flange ring on the hexagon slab. I mark the flange in its correct position by scoring on the hexagon surface along the inside edge of the flange. Then I turn the flange over, score it, and apply slurry. Scoring and slurry are also applied to the hexagon. (Figure 13) The flange is placed into position and pressure is applied to push out the extra slurry and make a seal. Then I cut away the inside of the hexagon flush against the flange wall (Figure 14), which forms the opening of the pot. (Figure 15) The edges of the top hexagon and the tops of the six sides of the pot are scored and slurried and the top hexagon is set in place. (Figure 16)

The piece at this stage of assembling is too moist to handle directly. I construct all my slab pieces on a plywood board. By placing another square of plywood on top of the piece, I am able to flip the

Figure 13. The flange is placed into position.

Figure 14. With a knife, the inside is cut away.

whole structure when necessary. (Figure 17) I now center the hexagon upside down on the wheel head and then visually set the foot in place. Next I draw a circle on the hexagon along the inside edge of the foot. This is done simply as a marker. I then turn the foot over and score the edge, making deep scratches in this case and brushing in the slurry. Finally I score the hexagon surface itself and replace the foot in position. Coiling is then placed on the inside and outside of the foot. I use coil as a bead on the outside of the foot because it helps the bond and establishes a nice curve in the shape of the seam. I round the bead of clay off with the same wooden tool used on the inside coils. (Figure 18)

I finish the outside edges by running a flat metal tool up all the rough seams. (Figure 19) Then with a damp sponge I run over the seam once or twice to get a smooth, clean look. (Figure 20)

The pot is now completely assembled and ready for decoration. Julie takes one of the completed hexagons and begins her opulent decorations.

Figure 15. The completed top of the pot is lifted off the wheel.

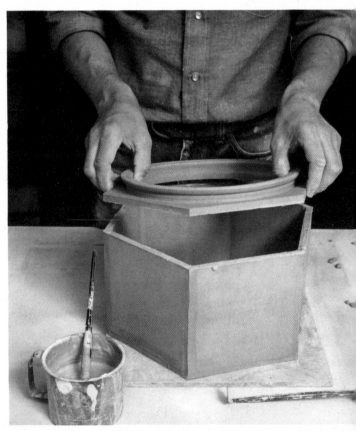

Figure 16. The top is set in place on the hexagon.

Figure 17. Plywood boards are used to turn the pot over.

Julie: During my days as a student at Wayne State I became intrigued by the coiling technique—so much so that I finished my graduate degree with an essay and study of coiling as a method of hand building. At that time my major interest was in developing the technique to lend freedom to a ceramic form. I was excited by natural forms, such as the outcroppings of stratified rock and the movement of waves along a beach; I was excited by the surfaces these forms created. My coil pots took on this feeling of movement and rough texture. My early pieces were very free-form and organic—much different from my recent pieces. I have moved from the free to the very controlled and symmetrical. No doubt I will swing back or possibly take a completely different direction as time goes by. But still the base of my expression in clay is the coil of clay and the desire on my part to make a statement with it.

Working with Ty on one of his hexagons is a new experience. We have talked about the idea for ages, but we needed the impetus of this book to get us started. I'm sure it will lead us into a whole series of pots that we'll do together. The slab pot has given me a new vehicle of expression; the flat sides lend themselves nicely to repeat patterns.

Figure 18. A wooden tool is used to form a smooth transition between the base and the foot.

Figure 19. A metal tool is used to smooth all joined edges.

Figure 20. A damp sponge is used to eliminate the tool marks.

I have never done coiling on slabs before, because I don't have the patience to construct slab pots—I always want to assemble them before the clay is ready and they end up sagging. I'm not sure why I have enough patience to sit for hours and roll coils but not enough to make slab pots, but I do know that Tyrone is exactly the opposite. He wouldn't make it past coil three! It's exciting that together we can create a piece that would not have been made by one of us alone. It becomes something of a third person.

Tyrone and I became involved with lusters several years ago. We started out by adding gold and platinum to our stoneware glazes and have now moved into using colored metallic lusters. As we have become more and more involved with colored lusters, I find my pots becoming more intricate and decorative. The brightness and glow allow me a range of colors that express totally different feelings in my pots. Where earlier I was limited to the "earthy" colors of stoneware glazes, I can now go wild with color.

When I was young my family never missed a circus or carnival; it's part of my nature to love bright colors and intricate patterns. Ty says I should have been a gypsy. Every time we attend an art fair I feel I've arrived! If you have ever arrived early at a fair, when all the vans are pulling in and everyone is shouting greetings, you will know what I mean. I enjoy selling our pots at fairs almost as much as I do making them. For me the culmination of the cycle comes when a person finds a piece he wants to take home and use or possibly treasure. Then the pots we make become more meaningful.

I have the love for color and pattern but I'm also a perfectionist— I learned that from Tyrone—so both color and pattern have to fit within my sense of organization. This characteristic has led me away from the freer forms into the more complex patterns of my recent pieces. I try to make statements in clay that "say it all," the way a circus wagon flashes an image on the imagination. I try to make my pots flash images. Most of my pieces are conceived with a specific image in mind, such as the Easter Egg Pot or Wedding Pot. The hexagon I decorate here already projects an image in the absolute beauty of its form, but I thoroughly enjoy embellishing that form.

I've worked out a system for doing repeat patterns with coils that works well and gives the finished piece unity. I begin by making a pattern piece. In this case I use a slab the size of a side of the hexagon. I experiment with designs on the slab until I find one that pleases me. I don't work well on paper. I have to do the planning in clay so that

I am able to visualize the results. The test piece also gives me a sample piece for experimenting with lusters if that becomes necessary. For this hexagon I have already decided to use only our white stoneware glaze with gold-lustered scrolls.

After I decide on the design, I measure the length of each different size scroll, and record the measurements—usually on the table where I'm working. I don't use a canvas-covered table, as the texture in the canvas leaves marks on the coils. I work directly on a sheet of unvarnished plywood. I also draw a measuring device, which resembles a ruler, directly on the tabletop. I have used rulers themselves but they have a way of disappearing. The tabletop measure can't either get away or get in the way.

I decorate with coils that I extrude from a Kemper clay tool. It's possible to roll out the coils by hand, but it's quicker to use the clay tool. Next I sponge down the coils to keep them soft and smooth and to stop possible cracking caused by the grog in the clay. Using my table ruler and list of measurements, I cut enough coils for one side of the pot. (Figure 21)

Because the coils are small they tend to dry out very quickly.

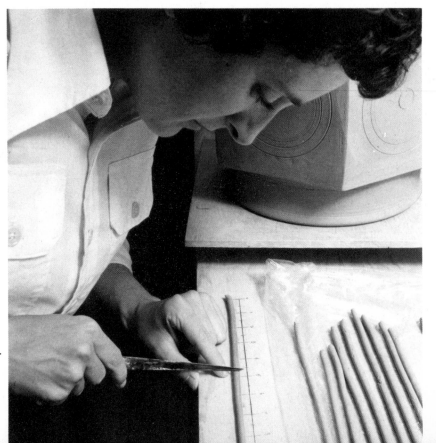

Figure 21. Coils are cut to predetermined measurements.

Figure 22. Coils are first formed into shape, then applied loosely to surface.

Figure 23. Coil and surface are scored, and then slurry is applied.

47

Figure 24. Pot is dipped into glaze until desired thickness forms.

If they are too dry they won't roll into curls but will simply crack in two. Therefore, I try to keep the coils on, and often covered with, a thin sheet of plastic. When all the coils are cut to length, I shape them into their final forms, keeping them on the plastic as much as possible. If the coils have remained fairly wet and the hexagon is leather hard, it is often possible to lay part of the decoration on the side without its falling off. And by keeping them loose at this point, I am able to go back over the scrolls and rearrange them so that they fit more precisely. (Figure 22)

(I should add that before Tyrone constructed the hexagon, I scribed circles in the flat slabs while they were centered on the wheel and spinning. These circles provide guidelines for my work and also add another dimension to the overall design.)

When one pattern of scrolls is in place, I lift the fat section of the scroll very carefully and scratch the pot surface with a needle tool. (Figure 23) Slurry is applied to both the hexagon and the coil. The coil is replaced and slight pressure is applied to assure a firm bond. The process is then repeated with each coil until the piece is finished. I decorate the lid in much the same way; however, I work out the design directly on it.

Once the coils have been applied, both pot and coils are allowed to dry very slowly. This is most important! If the coils dry before the slabs they will pop off the piece. To ensure that this won't happen, we wrap sheet plastic around the piece for several days. Gradually air is allowed to reach the clay. The total drying process may take as long as a week or two.

Doing this kind of decoration is a long, time-consuming job. This pot and most of my other recent pieces are labors of love, my personal statements in clay. I will probably never sell any of them. They are friends I enjoy having around. I love making them, and I love looking at the results.

When the two hexagons are completely dry they are bisque fired.

Bisque firing is a first or low firing. The piece is slowly heated in the kiln, along with many others, to Cone 07 (1800° F.). After this initial firing the clay has changed chemically to a hard state. It is now ready for glazing.

After the bisque firing the foot, flange, and underside of the lid are waxed. The hot wax is brushed on these surfaces while the piece is spinning on the wheel. Wax is applied to simplify the glazing process; it repels the liquid glaze and makes cleanup much faster and easier.

Next the pieces are glazed. White glaze is mixed in ten-gallon plastic cans. The quantity made from the following will last through a complete cycle of potting:

soda feldspar	434 grams
whiting	124 grams
kaolin	40 grams
flint	158 grams
bentonite	31 grams
ultrox	62 grams

The pots are glazed by a dip-and-pour method. The glaze is

poured into the interior sections and any excess is poured out. Because the bisqued pot is porous, the glaze is absorbed and a thick layer is retained on the surface. The exterior of the pot is dipped into the large container of glaze, completing the glazing process. (Figure 24)

The two hexagons are now fired in the kiln to Cone 10 (2300° F.). At this temperature the clay becomes dense and vitrified and the glaze forms a bond with the clay. When the pots are removed from the kiln the glaze is a smooth, shiny white.

The shiny white glaze becomes a base for the decals and lusters to be applied to Tyrone's hexagon. He begins with blue lusters, in bands on each side of the hexagon.

Lusters are metal-based colors that are suspended in an oil solution. Because of the oil base they are very slow to dry. They smear easily, and care must be taken to keep all surfaces clean and dust free. In order for Tyrone to luster-band all sides of his hexagon he must set the pot on its side in a shallow bowl. The pot rests on the four corners of each side, thus keeping the newly lustered sections in midair. The bowl and pot are centered on the kick wheel and the luster is banded on with a brush while the wheel is turning.

After the colored luster is applied to the sides, lid, and foot, the hexagon is placed in a small electric kiln and fired to Cone 018 (about 1300° F.). The oil burns away and the metallic luster fuses to the surface of the pot. The next process involves applying the ceramic decal. Tyrone is using a round decal taken from a portrait painted by Gainsborough. The decal is first soaked in water until it becomes loose from its protective backing. It is then slid into place on the pot and dried with a soft cloth. After all the decals are applied and thoroughly dry the gold luster is put on. The gold is similar to the colored lusters in that it is suspended in an oil base. The metal in this case is 23-karat gold.

The pot is again placed in the shallow bowl and centered on the kick wheel. The gold bands are applied as highlights at the edges of the colored luster and around the outside of all the circles. (Figure 25) After the banding is complete the pot is removed from the wheel and Tyrone finishes the lustering by covering the entire surface with gold luster. The pot is then returned to the kiln for a final (Cone 018) firing. In this firing the decal, composed of low-fired ceramic materials, and the gold luster fuse to form the jewellike surface on the finished piece.

My hexagon is now lustered, using a small brush and the same 23-karat gold luster. The scrolls of the decoration are carefully brushed with it, leaving the white of the stoneware glaze as the background color

Figure 25. Gold is banded on while pot is turning.

Figure 26. Gold luster is brushed on side.

of the pot. (Figure 26) This pot is also fired to Cone 018, which completes the process of decoration.

Achieving the jewellike quality of the finished pieces has taken both time and patience. Time for the Larsons is as much a part of the total process as carefully constructing the slabs or laboriously painting gold luster on the scrolls. The results they obtain can only be achieved by long hours of painstaking work.

And, too, the creative excitement they feel does not come from the spontaneous process of quickly forming a pot, but rather from the process leading up to and including the piece. The end result becomes most important. The Larsons do not measure the success of a pot by the time it takes to execute it. They judge, rather, the value of the time spent by the success of the resulting pot. In the case of the two hexagons, the Larsons feel they have used their time well; the resulting pieces please them and they hope the enjoyment they derived from creating them will be shared by others. —ED.

Wedding Jar, Julie Larson. 9″ high x 9″ wide

**Hexagonal
Gainsborough
Portrait Jar,** Tyrone
Larson. Blue
metallic luster,
decals, gold luster;
13″ high x 11″ wide

Butterfly Cube Jar, Tyrone
Larson. Colored metallic
lusters, decals, gold luster;
7″ high x 5″ wide x 5″ deep

Easter Egg Pot, Julie Larson.
Feldspatic stoneware glaze,
platinum, rose, and gold
lusters; 13″ high x 11″ wide

Hexagonal Canister Set, Tyrone Larson. White glaze, with cobalt and iron washes; overall dimensions, 11″ high x 23″ wide

Night Garden with Ladies
Jane Peiser

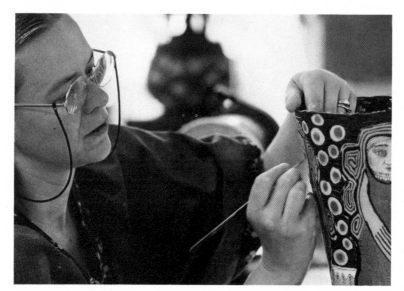

Jane Peiser's work is primitive in nature. It reflects the type of art she loves, an art that is very individual and special. She works in clay in new ways, and all her pieces are personal statements. In technique and design she is an artist doing unique work. The piece she has done for this book shows the millefiore *method, the first time this method for clay has been so clearly explained.*

Jane Peiser was born in Webster Groves, Missouri. She received her B.A. degree from George Peabody College for Teachers in Nashville, Tennessee, and her M.A. from the Institute of Design in Chicago.

Her work has been exhibited at the School of the Art Institute of Chicago, 1963; the University of Chicago, 1964; George Peabody College, 1965; Mundelein College, 1966; the Springfield Art Museum, 1967; Hanes Community Center, 1969; the Mint Museum of Art, 1970; the San Antonio Art Museum and the Asheville Art Museum, 1972; and the American Crafts Council, 1974.

Her work is now in the collections of Mrs. Oscar Marienthal, Mr. Bergman, and Dr. Solow, all of Chicago; Red Grooms of New York; the Mint Museum of Art in Charlotte, North Carolina; the University of Florida in Gainesville; and the Smithsonian Institution in Washington, D.C.

She has taught at New Trier High School in New Trier, Illinois, the Institute of Design in Chicago, and Penland School of Crafts. She lives in Penland, North Carolina.

Night Garden with Ladies. 12″ high x 8″ wide

I haven't always been a potter. I started out in art as a portrait painter. I thought at the time it was important to be a fine artist. So I decided to be a painter, but I didn't enjoy it. All the time, I know now, I should have been a craftsman.

I finally gave up portraits and began doing mosaics. I tiled everything in sight! I must have covered up a square mile. All kinds of stuff. But with mosaics I couldn't get the faces of the people. The eyeballs, for example, had to be square or hexangular. So I bought a kiln to make tiles of my own design.

One day I looked in the newspaper and found a kiln. I'm sure it is the only time in the history of the *Chicago Sun-Times* that a used kiln has been offered for sale. But it was in the newspaper for me. I fired those tiles I had made, but I never did mosaics again. From then on pottery has been my destiny!

I'm self-taught in ceramics. I have needed to find my own way with clay, learning by mistakes and luck, and from what the clay itself has to teach me. Clay is a wonderful material to work with. It is an inexpensive material that requires only a few tools for hand building. And the tools need only be household ones: rolling pins, forks, knives, and so on. There are also many possibilities with clay. It's a pliable and versatile material. One of the great pleasures I've found with clay is the many ways of approach that it offers. A million people can make a million different objects. About the only thing that is not possible with clay is the creation of transparencies.

Before coming to Penland I worked in relative isolation from professional craftsmen. I consider this a time of self-affirmation. I worked an average of twelve hours a day and grew in proficiency, but most of all I grew in my own personal style. Finding my own way with clay was easier for me because I was out of touch with other current potters and schools of pottery.

In my opinion, only technical aspects should be taught in schools. Once they are mastered, students should be left alone to make what they really want to make and not be influenced to make what is the current acceptable style. But I have lost some in not going to school. I'm lacking in technical know-how, which I've had to learn on my own—all the complex chemistry of glazes and clays.

The real problem with colleges and art schools is that they're part of the establishment and they tend to teach people to work within safe esthetic limits. It takes ten years to get over that—if one ever gets over it—and do one's own work.

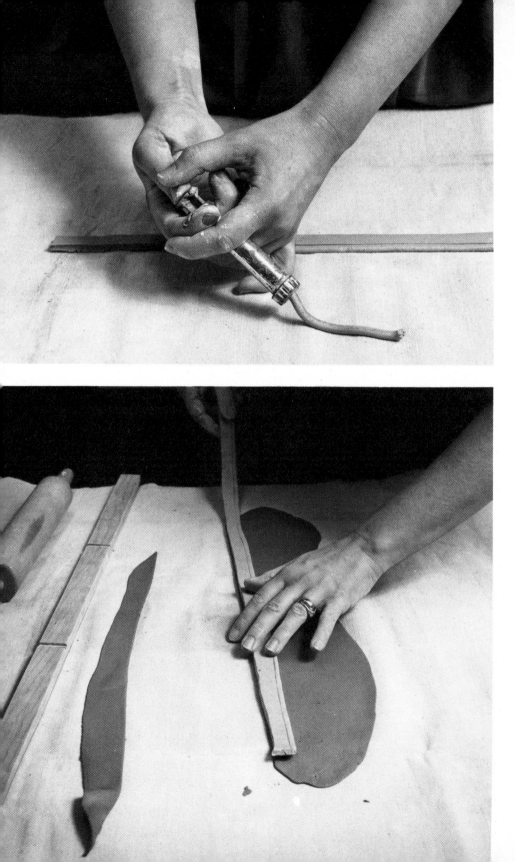

Figure 1. The clay for the fingers is extruded.

Figure 2. Black clay is placed around each finger.

The juried shows, too, are responsible for the lack of variety in pottery from person to person. Whenever a person's work is to be judged, he is constrained from being outlandish or personal. One is then not very lucky if one's work is really unique and different from what is being done. A great price is paid for striking out on one's own, but it's very satisfying to know you have been honest. There is also less distance between your work and yourself.

My own work is very individualistic. It may not be technically perfect, and I don't think it's wonderful in design, and there are other drawbacks to it, but all the pieces are uniquely mine and that's very important to me as a craftsman.

What I do in clay can be made on a card table in the kitchen. It is not that difficult. And not a lot of space is required. I worked for years on the back porch of our home in Chicago. Much of what I do can be fired in an electric kiln, which can be run off household current. The only limitation is in the size of what can be made—a big kiln cannot be heated on 110 current.

I like to make utilitarian objects that people can use; I rarely make things that can't be. If a person can't use it, then it becomes art and it becomes much too serious. I don't think of my works as pieces of art,

Figure 3. The fingers before they are added to the arm and then to the *millefiore*.

Figure 4. The first arm is added.

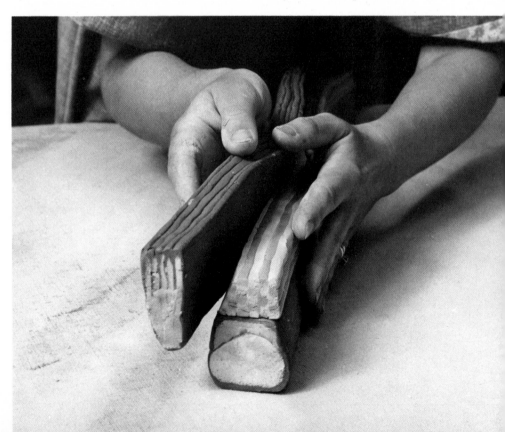

nor do I think of myself as making essentially useless objects whose only reason to be is their beauty. I am a producing potter making a living from my work. My aim in making pots is to make something people will like well enough to keep and use.

I've always enjoyed building my pots by hand without the use of a wheel—I have very little liking for perfectly rounded hollow shapes. And I've always liked to build with coils. I haven't changed much in outlook over the years—just progressed in skill.

Most people in ceramics work with earthy colors and without images on their pots, but I've always loved to make things with bright colors, and all my pots have some recognizable subject matter. Abstraction to me is not real, and design alone does not interest me. My work is primitive in nature—I greatly admire primitive paintings, especially Persian and Indian miniature paintings.

Six years after I began to make pots, my husband Mark and I moved to Penland, where we now live. At Penland I met many skilled and talented production potters from whom I've learned much, and I was encouraged to use the school's equipment, mainly its gas-fired salt and reduction kilns.

The new equipment and materials greatly inspired me. It came at

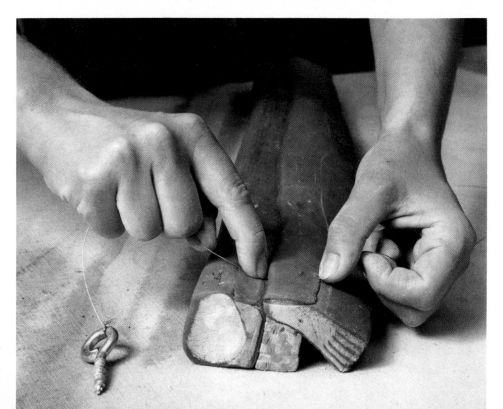

Figure 5. The first arm is trimmed.

Figure 6. The second arm is added.

Figure 7. Three colors are laminated together for the hair.

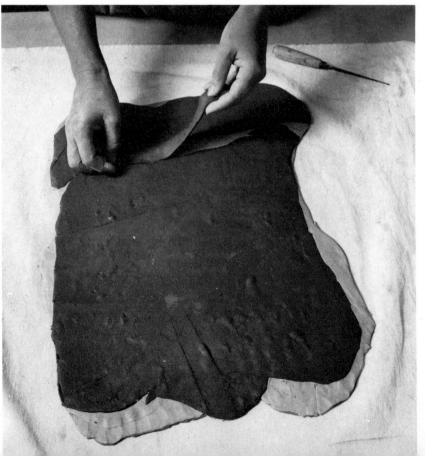

Figure 8. The first piece of hair is added.

a time when I longed for a more competent look in my work. I am grateful to Penland School of Crafts for this opportunity. Many accomplished craftsmen at Penland helped me, particularly Judy Cornell, now at the Archie Bray Foundation.

I worked successfully at Penland until Martha, our child, was born. Before the baby I could stay up all night and work, but no longer. That meant I wasn't producing as much, and without pots, I couldn't go to shows and fairs. It became very frustrating. One has to have a tremendous will, once one has a family, to get somewhere in pottery and yet not spoil life for everyone else.

I don't like to make plain pots. I buy them and appreciate them, but I want my own pots to be highly decorative, and that takes a long time to do with a brush.

Figure 9. The checkered fabric of the skirt is added.

Figure 10. The finished *millefiore*.

I've been helped in achieving this intricacy by using the *millefiore* technique. This is an old glass technique I learned from my husband, who is a glassblower. Similar methods have often been used in clay.

Millefiore is a marvelous way of getting a very rich surface decoration on a pot without having to sit down and laboriously do it with a brush, as I had done in the past. It's also nice because I've gotten new images by using the technique. I've been doing it for over a year and I'm just now reaching the point where it looks the way I want.

Making a *millefiore* is the beginning process; it's a long process that I do not enjoy, but it's one of the things that has to be done in order to achieve a beautiful end result. I find that the closer the pot is to being finished, the more I enjoy working on it.

The *millefiore* also allows me to do a series of different kinds of pots. When I was doing portraits, I envied painters who could do eight or ten paintings of the same thing and really get into a subject. I was lucky to be able to do just one painting. Now, with the *millefiore*, I can get an idea and do a whole series of things. I can make up different *millefiores* and use parts of all of them for one pot.

Making a *millefiore* is very much like making ice-box cookies. By that, I mean I make a roll, or loaf, and slice it, and use the slices on the sides of the pots. It takes me anywhere from a half hour to twenty hours to make a *millefiore*. The pot itself takes from one to three hours to make. I then need another half hour to sand the pot and between two and six hours to China-paint it. I then fire the pot three different times.

I begin the process with white clay. The basic formula is Judy Cornell's porcelain throwing body, with sand added.

PORCELAIN	CONE 9–CONE 10
grolleg clay	55 pounds
potash feldspar	20 "
flint	12 "
pyrofilite	13 "
bentonite	2 (per 100-pound batch)

Bentonite is only for new clay. After the clay has aged the use of bentonite is unnecessary. Four to five percent sand can be added. Also .5 percent Fiberglas strands for greater flexibility in hand building. One cup of additive "A," a wood extract compound, added to a hundred pounds of dry mix adds dry strength before firing.

White clay produces the brightest colors. I start with this white

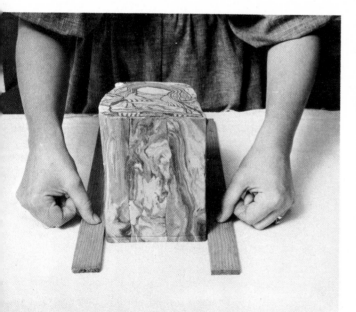

Figure 11. A slice of the *millefiore* is cut off to make a pot.

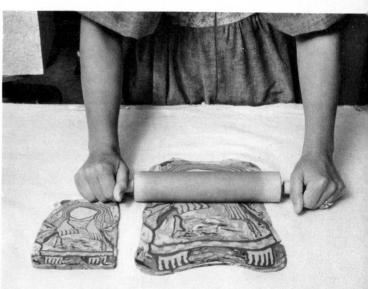

Figure 12. The slice is rolled out to approximately 1/16 inch.

Figure 13. The slices are taped to the inside surface of a mold to hold them in place while pot is built.

clay and add oxides and body stains to color them. I also run tests in my clay coloring, which I do this way: I first mix the dry clay ingredients thoroughly by pouring them back and forth from one bucket to another. Then I weigh out the correct percentage of oxide and add it to the clay. I sift this mixture into water and let it settle. Next I pour off the excess water and pour the resulting clay slip onto plaster to remove enough water to make the clay workable.

The following percentages added to white clay body and glazed will more than likely produce these colors. Tests should always be run before any large amounts of clay are mixed:

Figure 14. Small design pieces are made to be added as the pot is built.

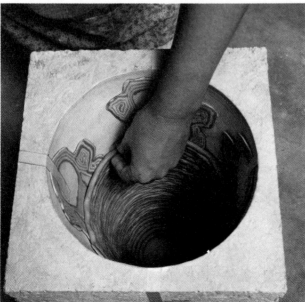

Figure 15. The pot is built up from coils.

pink	8% commercial pink stain
yellow	8% commercial yellow stain
green	$\frac{1}{2}$% green chrome oxide
yellow	8% rutile
black	2% cobalt oxide and 7% iron chromate
lavender	5% pink stain and $\frac{1}{2}$% cobalt carbonate
blue	$\frac{1}{2}$% to 1% cobalt carbonate
brown	3% red iron oxide

Before beginning to make a *millefiore*, I make a color sketch of the figure or object that I want, which is helpful as a guide.

The *millefiore* shown here is built from the inside of the roll out. I begin by rolling out the pink clay of the fingers. (Figure 1) I stretch the clay by turning it over between rollings. (Of course, it is necessary when working with clay to keep it damp at all times, so when I'm not working with the loaf, I wrap it in plastic to maintain the moisture.) Each element is built separately and packed tightly to the other components. (Figures 2–6) Air pockets are pricked out as I work; this also keeps the clay firm. The *millefiore* is built in this sequence: face, dress, arms, hair, skirt, feet.

The hair is added near the end. I make it from three separate layers. of clay, and top it with black clay. (Figure 7) I like having black lines around everything in my work, though I'm not sure why. Maybe when I was a little girl I colored a lot of coloring books. The hair is made of dark yellow, a lighter yellow, then topped with black (Figure 8). I like pretty hair and it is usually an exaggerated and stylized part of all my figures. Finally the checkered fabric of the skirt is added. (Figure 9)

Once the *millefiore* loaf is finished I let it sit overnight so the whole loaf gains the same degree of wetness. (Figure 10) There's one thing that cannot be done with clay: you can't place a dry piece and a wet piece together and have them stay together, because clay shrinks as it dries. That's probably one of its biggest problems. Always try to work with clays that have the same degree of moisture. When I'm not using the *millefiore* I keep plastic around it. That way I can keep it for months, until I've used it all up.

I cut the slices according to how large a form I want. I cut them thin if I want the form small, thicker for bigger pieces. If I want to make a smaller pot and use this figure, I take part of the loaf and pound it into a smaller diameter, then I slice it off. It's extremely versatile.

When the *millefiore* is salted, it changes colors, depending on whether it is oxidized or reduced in the kiln. I have about twenty basic

Figure 16. The inside is pressed firmly against the outside design, and smoothed.

Figure 17. A finished pot, another in the series, is removed from the mold.

Figure 18. When it is bone dry, the surface of the finished pot is sanded.

colors that I work with, but some colors I cannot get because the temperature of the kiln is too high. The higher the temperature, the more colors will burn out.

By pushing the *millefiore* form I can distort the image. To me that's a great advantage, for one *millefiore* can take on many different appearances.

To cut the *millefiore* I draw a tight wire through the loaf. (Figure 11) I use two slats as guideposts, and the thickness of the slats determines the thickness of the slice. It is very important to keep the wire tight to make sure the thickness of the slice remains the same through the cut. This is a standard slab-cutting technique.

The slices are next rolled out with a rolling pin. (Figure 12) They will stretch and flatten to the size I want. Again, I have to turn them over and over continually, rolling the slice down each time. When they are particularly thin slices, I turn them with two pieces of cloth. They handle much easier this way.

The slices of the *millefiore* are then placed in a plaster mold that I've made out of No. 1 molding plaster. Plaster is a good material for potters because it takes up water. I place the figures into the mold and hold them in place with masking tape. (Figure 13) I make some extra design elements which I will add as the pot is built up. (Figure 14)

In order to use a *millefiore* it must be adhered to the surface of the pot. This must be done by laying the *millefiore* on a surface and pressing slabs of coils against the *millefiore* from behind. (Figure 15) Any concave surface, preferably made of plaster, may be used. For my own work, I've found that it is best to use a mold for the entire piece, which must be left in the mold until it is stiff enough to remove without distorting the shape. This usually means a twenty-four-hour drying period. A convex surface cannot be used, as the clay shrinks in drying and will crack on the convex plaster shape.

When I am finished coiling this pot, it will be about sixteen inches tall. However, after firing, it will measure only thirteen inches, due to shrinkage. Once the clay is in the mold, I smooth it out on the inside. This is necessary to hold all the parts together. (Figure 16)

I then leave the pot for twenty-four hours to dry before removing it from the mold. (Figure 17) The pot has to be dried slowly and carefully once it is taken from the mold. Again, I keep mine wrapped in plastic. For one or two hours each day—for the next two weeks—I remove it from the plastic and let it dry. If a pot dries quickly it will dry unevenly, and if it dries unevenly it will crack.

Figure 19. The face on another pot in the series is painted in before the final firing.

Once the pot is bone dry it is sanded and bisqued. (Figure 18) I bisque to Cone 06 in an electric kiln. Then I line the inside with glaze, and I paint a second glaze on the white areas outside the pot that I want to China-paint. (Figure 19) I use two different glazes:

INSIDE LINER C 7 CELADON		OUTSIDE: SEMI-MATTE OPAQUE WHITE (TEMPLE WHITE)	
K 200 potash feldspar	700 grams	K 200 feldspar	346 grams
whiting	100 ″	dolomite	195 ″
kaolin	100 ″	whiting	27 ″
Gersttey borate	100 ″	K.P. kaolin	224 ″
flint	100 ″	flint	198 ″
	1100 ″	bentonite	20 ″
1% or 2% red iron oxide	11 ″		1010 grams
	1111 grams		

The inside glaze is poured into the pot, while the outside one is brushed on.

I next load the piece in my salt kiln and fire the kiln to Cone 10. I throw in about five quarts of rock salt to salt-glaze the outside, then I take it out and China-paint (or overglaze) the areas that are blank.

The images I China-paint are of women, animals, flowers, and plants. I have definite feelings about the faces and figures. Some of my people I'd like to know, while some seem to be weak and empty; there are other figures that seem strong, but not very nice. Generally, though, I have people on my pots who are strong yet slightly naive—the kind of people I like.

Regardless of the size of the pot, I work on a small scale. All my faces are miniature and have great detail. I think that I'm unsuccessful with large drawings. No matter how big the pot is, I'm always working—at least in my mind—in one-inch squares. That's another reason why it takes me so long to do a piece.

Before beginning to China-paint, I wash the area in alcohol to make sure the oil from fingerprints is cleaned off. I also mix the China paint with a commercial medium that is oily and will adhere to the surface of a vitreous pot.

I apply China paint with a brush; and I think brushing it on is one of its virtues. I then fire the China painting to Cone 017 in my electric kiln. In order to fire correctly I leave the lid up until the oil finishes burning out. After this firing, my pot is complete.

Noah's Ark. Cone 6, with glaze stains, oxidation; 15″ high x 6½″ wide

Opposite page: **Medieval Clock.** Cone 10, porcelain reduction with overglaze, decoration at Cone .017; 22" high x 14" wide

Tipton Family Graveyard. Cone .06, underglazed; 17" high x 11½" wide

Girls in Bed. Cone 10, porcelain, color clay, salted overglaze added at Cone .017; 7½" high x 8½" wide

Man with Blinders
Tom Suomalainen

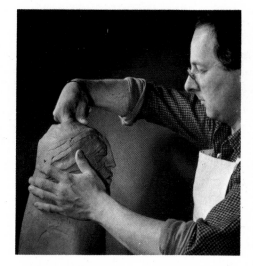

Tom Suomalainen is an artist who works in many diverse forms, but primarily in ceramics. His work is never predictable and continually surprises the viewer. It is always closely related to nature forms, colors, and textures. Much of his work has its germination in drawings that are recorded in his journal, and often an idea for a clay form will have its origin in a sketch done years before. He is well known for his hand-built pieces, such as the "Man with Blinders" that he has done for this book.

Tom Suomalainen was born in Duluth, Minnesota. He received his B.A. degree from the University of Minnesota in Duluth and his M.F.A. from Tulane University in New Orleans. His work has been exhibited at Greenwich House in New York, 1969; the Gallery of Contemporary Art in Winston-Salem, North Carolina, and The Arts in Chapel Hill, North Carolina, 1970; as part of the New Jersey Craftsmen at the Fairtree Gallery in New York, and at Columbia University, the Michael Schwerner Memorial Fund, in New York, 1973.

His work appears in the collections of Mr. and Mrs. Ira Julian of Winston-Salem, North Carolina, and of Mr. and Mrs. John Thibaut of Chapel Hill, North Carolina.

He has taught at the Arts and Crafts Association of the Arts Council and at North Carolina Governors School, Salem College, both in Winston-Salem, North Carolina; High Point College in High Point, North Carolina; the Memphis Academy of Arts in Memphis, Tennessee; Cooper Square Art Center in New York; and Penland School of Crafts. He lives in Walnut Cove, North Carolina.

Man with Blinders I. Oxidation-fired at Cone 9 with underglaze slips; 23" high x 8" wide x 6½" deep

Recalling first experiences with clay takes me back to my grandfather's homestead in Minnesota. All of us kids, running naked, would slosh and climb our way through a watery swamp. Squealing with delight, we would splash water on the mud slides, grease up with sticky mud, and slide into slow-moving Floodwood River. In the river we would moor ourselves to deadheads and live in the world of our imagination. My formative years in the country of Minnesota seem to have foretold—or, rather, shaped—a life for me that is alive to the elements and the pleasures of the sensuous eye, since I early felt a relation to materials responsive to my hands.

My life seems to be filled with dramas and fantasies. It is good that I have found clay to give shape to the fantasies; I can now mesh them with a more temperate concern for form, texture, and color harmonies as found in nature.

The struggle to establish an identity while in a then seemingly remote high school is common to many, and not particularly unique in view of these changing times. The fifties were *the* years, as my generation professes! Commencement for me was moving to Duluth and attending the University of Minnesota, beginning first as a geology major and then quickly and intuitively changing to a curriculum in the creative arts.

Glenn C. Nelson guided my hands the four years I studied there. His gentle concern and respect for individual interests gave me a learning experience in clay that, though directed to pottery and the influence of Scandinavian ceramic design, was extremely diverse. The struggle to learn a craftsman's skill was eased by his jovial and patient nature. And the tools for learning were always available in both his studio and his home. I recall many an evening enjoying some aquavit and listening to Glenn joyfully tell of his last trip to Denmark or Helsinki, as he shared his slides with us—of countrysides and studios and ceramic factories remote from our own experience.

My last two years at Minnesota were concentrated in the creative arts and art history. Working as Nelson's lab assistant gave me additional time in the ceramics studio, but I was also painting, drawing, and working in graphics. As slide librarian for the art history department I literally had at my fingertips the history of man's civilization as represented in the arts. The impact of these historical documents is still overwhelming to me and has brought me to realize that everything I make is a total statement of my person at the time it is created.

The Minnesota climate is one that requires inborn stamina. The seasons are very distinct and emotional. The winters are long and cold;

Figure 1. The slabs are cut with a wire; thickness is not a major consideration.

the summers are brief. But for graduate school I went south to Louisiana.

The climate of New Orleans is in dramatic contrast to Minnesota. Traveling along the Mississippi River proved to be an experience of the senses. Traveling over unknown terrain made me wish I'd studied more geology, but this was secondary to the visual bombardment of landscapes. They would have kept me painting and drawing by the roadsides for months, had I not stepped on the accelerator in hope of reaching a cool spot in the hot August sun. New Orleans, the sensual experience, seemed to be unraveling my Scandinavian armor!

While at Tulane I quickly learned that my mind and body weren't ready for the discipline of becoming a potter who produced entirely utilitarian wares. Dirk Hubers, as my friend and ceramics professor, was aware of my changing person and encouraged me to pursue the use of clay as a medium of personal expression.

Pre-Columbian history brought me to an awareness of the many roles clay has played in human civilization. People have built homes with clay, they have eaten off plates made from it, they have created images of their gods with it. For nearly every civilization, clay has been a primary natural resource, providing material for anything from drinking cups to bathtubs to religious icons!

For a short period I thought of myself as having a restrictive viewpoint on many subjects. It is as if I was going straight ahead without giving consideration to other points of view. Out of this feeling has come "Man with Blinders."

I have never felt hampered by the concept of clay as strictly a pottery material. Nor do I object to being called a potter, because that is true in a historical sense. But I think the term my grandfather used in reference to me is more applicable. Once, when he was about eighty, and I was trying to explain to him what my work was like, he finally came up with the Finnish words *savi nikkari*, which mean "clay carpenter." He felt I was a clay carpenter because I was making angular and asymmetrical forms that were not necessarily functional or turned on the potter's wheel.

The piece I am making here is hollow and has tiny holes in the bottom sides to allow the air and heat to circulate so that the pieces will dry and fire evenly. In the actual features—the eyes and mouth— there will be air spaces also; they are a structural consideration.

The clay I use is a low-iron salt clay with extra silica. I am continually experimenting with clay bodies, as clays vary and that variance is related to the forms the clay takes. The clay bodies I use in Cone 9 salt firing are variations of these two formulas:

1.	A.P. Green fireclay	45
	Jordan stoneware	20
	Cedar Heights red	5
	ball clay	10
	Avery kaolin	5
	soda feldspar	10
	silica	10
	grog as desired	
2.	A.P. Green fireclay	35
	Jordan stoneware	35
	Cedar Heights red	5
	ball clay	10
	Avery kaolin	10
	potash feldspar	5
	silica	5
	grog as desired	

These clays will probably need individual adjustments, since I made them only from materials in my inventory. My clays always vary, as I am not an accurate measurer and I use a lot of slaked clay of unknown composition, primarily a high-content fireclay body I mixed in quantity that was not responding well. I don't mind taking chances!

The process transformation of clay is astounding! The clay is dug out of the ground, or compounds are made of different clays; it is soft at first, but then firms up as it is worked. In drying it becomes brittle and fragile. With bisque firing the clay is transformed from a plastic material to a refractory. With stoneware-reduction glaze firing it is often difficult to reconnect with the bisqued piece. If the piece seems foreign to my experience, or the emotional connection while glazing does not come spontaneously, I let the piece stand in the studio until I feel in touch. Recently, salt firing, as a once-fired process, has eliminated this separation and involved me more dramatically with the firing because the timing and temperature affect the pieces to a stronger degree as to texture, flashings, and exact color variations.

Since the salt firings are dependent on the way in which salt vapors pass through the kiln, many variations can occur in a single firing. Some spots are hotter or cooler or on either the windward or leeward

Figure 2. The slabs are rolled out from corner to corner.

of the flames. Experiments using clay "caps" over pieces or placing pieces in pierced saggers have brought unexpected and beautiful results. Much more experimentation with clay bodies and cycles of firing will surely change my forms, just as they change in relation to a continually changing process.

For this piece, the slabs are cut freehand from a wedged block of clay with a wire. (Figure 1) I make no measurements. Thickness is variable, but in rolling out later, compensations can be made. Also, the textured surface can be smoothed on one side, leaving the imprint of the canvas on the other.

The thick slabs dry on edge: this allows for the greatest air circulation around them. When stiffened, the slabs are rolled from corner to corner, which keeps them rectangular—more or less. (Figure 2) I watch what is happening to the clay as it moves, at each roll. My hands are feeling the clay through the wood of the roller. The clay softens gradually as it is rolled.

Working with clay is a tactile experience, and there is no part of the process that isn't part of the whole. What my feet are standing on, the canvas, the paper, how the table feels, how the clay feels—all are part of the experience. So is the heat in the room and the sweat.

The base shape is cut to fit the wooden bat. (Figure 3) The general shape has been determined. Once I have the base and the first section of walls up I can start visualizing the total form. The proportions of the base are like the foundation of a house. Once you make that commitment, everything done must be in relation to that first single move.

The slabs are scored and joined together with a fork. (Figure 4) The total fork meshes the clay together, nearly pushing through the clay wall. I don't use any slip. If I used slip the paddle or roller would stick while I was reshaping the corners. The clay should remain medium soft, not sticky at the seams.

I rarely make a single pot at a time; they develop as part of a series. There will be two or three or six, depending on size. It is too much work to do just one piece; and when I am in the rhythm of work it is easier to do them together. I don't want to stop the creative process by having to prepare more materials. The working rhythm, though sporadic, is cyclical.

Figure 4. The slabs are joined by scoring with a fork.

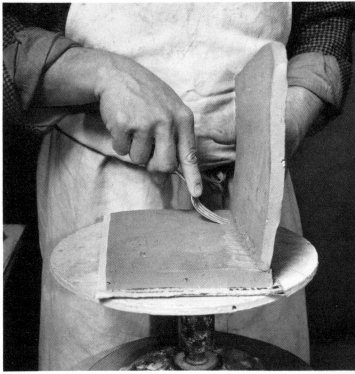

Figure 3. The base is fitted to the wooden bat.

Figure 5. Coils are pressed into the corners of the slabs.

Figure 6. The corners are defined with a rolling pin.

When I am working on several pieces, the softer ones can grow more slowly. Each section of slabs is built up, sometimes using scraps to fill in. Inside, coils are smoothed into the corners for added strength. (Figure 5) I like the inside finished. If the pieces were to break, I'd like to know that my work was finished on the inside.

Although the pieces are made in series they are never the same; they change as my mood changes. From morning to night my mood is reflected in the faces or features of the pieces. I may be reflective or happy or troubled, and that feeling will be transferred to the clay.

The only preconceived notions I have about any piece are due to the actual physical limitations of the size of the kiln or the space available to me in other potters' kilns. When I was working in New Jersey there was an occasion on which pieces outgrew my kiln and I had to transport the raw pieces in the back of my pickup truck to Toshiko Takaezu's studio. Transporting four-foot pieces is done with great trepidation, but I have yet to break a large piece in handling.

As the pieces progress there is much variety in surface texture, from scoring, forking, paddling, mashing the clay together. Paddling smoothes out some texture but leaves the corner lines clear.

It is possible to redefine the corner lines or angles with a rolling pin. (Figure 6) The vertical piece needs a strong unwavering line from the base to the top so that the eye doesn't stray from the continuous vertical thrust. The clay textures that are left slow the eye and add surface dimension that is enhanced later with salt firing.

I spend a lot of time studying the piece when it is two-thirds finished. Each angle is studied and responded to in relation to the other parts. Often, to soften the hard rectangular form, the upper portion is rolled on the corner with the rolling pin to make the portion just below the head into an oval form.

While I am thinking about the head form I roll out coils of various thicknesses and cover them with a dampened cloth to keep them moist until the final spurt of energy comes and I finish the piece. The only time I score and slip the pieces is when they sit unfinished overnight or when there is a long lapse in my working rhythm. A layer of plastic firmly folded over the top edge keeps the clay moist longer.

With the exception of some utilitarian pieces my work almost always has some sort of figuration in it. For me, that is the human element as it relates to nature. The spirit and energy of birds have also meshed with figurations for me, or have become forms in themselves. Shore birds and geese have a stance and smoothness that my hands like to form. The sound of migrating geese reaches the remote, elusive sense of seasonal perception that evokes the mystery of migration, and the act of migration awakens things unknown in me. Perhaps it gives me a greater sense of location.

The egg, as well, has become for me an important series of forms. The symbolism of the egg is manifold, but what is most relevant to me is the energy of the form. I am interested in the idea of seeds and the process of germination. I eat many sprouted foods—lentils, beans, alfalfa—and while handling and eating them I enjoy their beauty and freshness, which is part of their organic nature. The process of growing

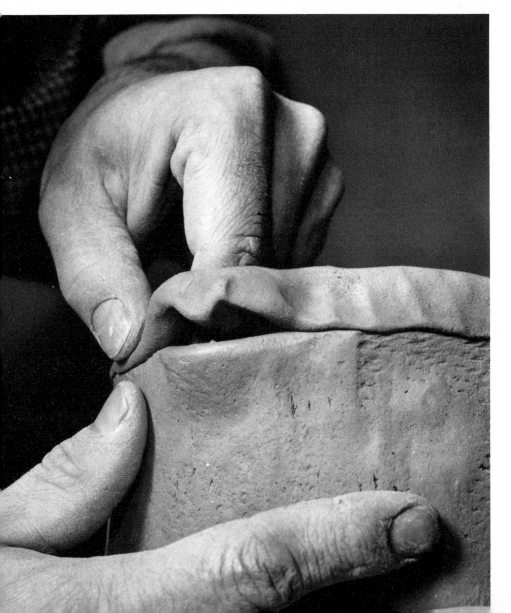

Figure 7. The face-head is built with the arrangement of coils.

Figure 8. Teeth are arranged for structural purposes. They keep the mouth open as the weight of the coils presses down.

my own food is inseparable from my work. In one way or other, my hands are in clay—red North Carolina clay.

The face-head form is built upward, from the chin to the mouth, teeth, cheeks, nose, eyes, and then to the crown of the head. My faces are not visual self-portraits, but they do express what I am feeling at the time. I think of them as geography, for the faces are built out of clay strata. (Figure 7)

Besides being expressive, the teeth are included for structural reasons. They keep the mouth open, as sometimes the weight of the coils above tends to press the lips down. (Figure 8)

As the piece nears completion I look inside and wonder if the inside space should be accessible or if it should be closed off. There is quite a difference. Recently I've become concerned with using interior space for grain storage. But with this piece it isn't necessary; it is an object that does not call for definition as a container. (Figure 9, a–f)

The final step is to make the blinders. I cut one-inch lengths of clay coil and press them into the shape I want. I score and slip the sides of the head and press the blinders into place, moving them around several times before I find just the right position.

Since I touched clay formally for the first time, in 1957, the clay forms I have used have gone through a long and continuous growing process. However, my forms and glazes have consistently remained organic and a part of my moods in response to the harmonies of nature. Color changes particularly reflect the seasons, and many of my glazes resemble the textures and colors of water, stream beds, the bark of trees, mosses and leaves, the sky, and geographical terrain.

The last phase in completing a piece is subjecting it to the fire. It is at this point that the emotional and physical handling of the clay and glazes reaches total fulfillment. Firings are variable for many reasons. No forms ever repeat themselves exactly, and even in a related series of work the arrangement of kiln furniture is never standardized. And stacking each kiln is a new experience. Recalling that certain portions of the kiln receive more flame than others and that certain places usually are either lightly or heavily salted, you must give special consideration to each piece as you place it among the growing number of pieces in the kiln. Relationships because of heights and widths must be carefully considered, taking into account air currents and salting patterns and economical use of available space.

In salt firing/glazing I am glazing the pieces with the brick wall of the kiln separating me from the work. But experience, hope, and

Figure 9. The building of the face and head. The expression of the face is achieved by manipulating the coils.

a

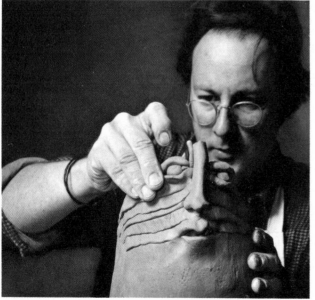

b

c

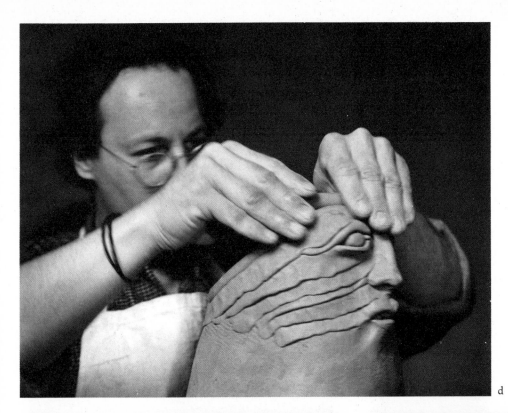

d

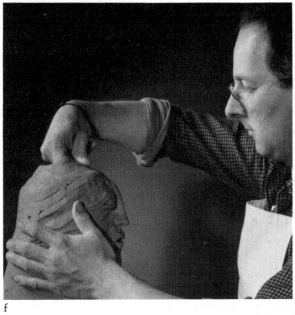

e   f

imagination penetrate the bricks and handfuls of salt nourish the flames.

After Cone 9 is over, table salt, granular salt, or rock salt in various combinations and timings is thrown into the kiln through the salting ports at approximately twenty- to forty-minute intervals. Dampers are opened and closed, the kiln oxidizes and reduces, in a rhythm that seems to be established by my own feelings about the strength or fragility of the work and the way the wind is blowing and whether the sky is cloudy or clear. I prefer clear days for firing (the kiln is outdoors), as they seem to provide a calming atmosphere that best guides both the kiln and me through the firing cycle.

Trying to describe the interrelatedness of my lifestyle and my work can best be explained this way. It is like my habit of walking at night, even on the darkest nights, relying only on the sensitivity of my feet to find the path and sense the proximity of my surroundings so that I avoid bumping into the elements of the forest. The beginning clay forms are the paths followed by the sensitivity of my hands. Each piece is a document of that particular walk.

It was not until 1967, when I came to Penland to teach a summer session and subsequently stayed as a resident craftsman for two years, that I had the opportunity to fully combine a geographical location, a physical plant, and an emotional environment into a direct clay-working experience that was not academically related. This experience came at a time when the prospect of remaining in the academic world as a teacher was against my sensibilities. In retrospect, I know that at Penland I had in two years completely and irreversibly changed commitments. Teaching commitments since then have been short term and relative to places and people that were close to me. They have been in Eads, Tennessee, at Cynthia Bringle's studio; in Manhattan; in Clinton, New Jersey, at Toshiko Takaezu's studio; in Asbury, New Jersey, with a close friend; and, just prior to coming back to North Carolina, at Byron Temple's studio in Lambertville, New Jersey. Along with these friends and others, as with Glenn and Dirk, I have been able to share experiences and concepts that I have integrated with my own directions. And in many ways, these concepts are germinating and nourishing still undefined forms, textures, and colors.

The work represented in this book reflects only a portion of the many forms that have grown in the studios I have worked in. However, it does reflect a form that has been part of a series, which began at Penland in the winter of 1968 and, I suspect, will continue as part of an ever changing, but always recurring, form.

Seer. Salt-reduction-fired at Cone 9; 13″ high x 3″ wide x 5″ deep

Opposite page: **Bearer.** Salt-glazed in oxidation atmosphere at Cone 9; white slip sprayed on face; 12$\frac{3}{4}$" high x 5$\frac{1}{8}$" wide x 6" deep

Dead Letter Box. Salt-glazed in oxidation atmosphere at Cone 9; 9$\frac{1}{4}$" high x 5$\frac{3}{4}$" wide x 8" deep

Man with Blinders II. Salt-reduction-fired at Cone 9; Albany slip glaze with brushed salt slips and oxides of black iron oxide and rutile; 24$\frac{1}{2}$" high x 6$\frac{1}{2}$" wide x 8" deep

Arch
Bruno LaVerdiere

Bruno LaVerdiere has worked in nearly all artistic forms, from line drawings to stained-glass windows. He is best known as a sculptor, and his pieces of art are large and powerful statements. For this book he has created a seven-foot arch to show that truly large pieces can be made from the soft material of clay.

Bruno LaVerdiere was born in Waterville, Maine. He received his education at Saint John's University in Collegeville, Minnesota; the University of Washington in Seattle; Saint Martin's College in Olympia, Washington; and the Art Students' League in New York.

He has had solo exhibitions at Scarabeus, Ltd. in New York and the Collectors' Gallery in Bellevue, Washington, 1964; the State Capitol Museum in Olympia, Washington, 1965; the Lee Nordness Gallery in New York, 1971; the Friends of the Crafts Gallery in Seattle, 1972; the Cheney Cowles Museum in Spokane, Washington State College in Pullman, Washington, and the Sculpture House in New York, 1973; the Schenectady Museum in Schenectady, New York, and the Hyde Collection in Glens Falls, New York, 1974.

His work appears in the collections of the Cheney Cowles Museum in Spokane; the Everson Museum of Art in Syracuse, New York; the Johnson Wax Collection (Objects USA); the Monson Collection in the Museum of Art, San Francisco; and the Prieto Memorial Collection at Mills College, Oakland, California.

He has taught at Greenwich House Pottery, Penn State University, Scripps College, Saint Martin's College, and Penland School of Crafts. He lives in Hadley, New York.

Arch. 7′ 3″ high x 4′ wide

I became involved with art in 1955 when I joined a Benedictine monastery in Olympia, Washington. The monastery was my first patron. I had no formal training in art until they sent me to college—Saint John's University in Minnesota—where I studied art full time for a year. That was in 1957, and for the next ten years, until I left the monastery, I was its unofficial artist-in-residence.

The title "artist-in-residence" is a bit pretentious for what I did. I was primarily a monk, but I worked at all sorts of things in the general realm of art, from carving tombstones to making stained-glass windows. I did all the art repair work at the monastery and at the college it operated. Any unfamiliar techniques I learned by myself—they would give me a job to do and I'd solve any problems by doing research in the library.

During this time I also set up a studio and began to do pottery. I thought of pottery then as something to be done between major works, but I started to show my ceramics and gradually built something of a reputation on the West Coast.

In 1965 the monastery sent me to New York City for two years to study further at the Art Students' League—sculpture and anatomy in particular—and I also taught in the Village at Greenwich House Pottery. While in New York I began to concentrate intensively on sculpture, experimenting with a great variety of materials. At that time, too, I first heard about Penland School of Crafts, from Toshiko Takaezu, and in 1967, after I left the monastery, I went to Penland to teach. I went to Penland for three summers thereafter as an instructor. I'm presently living in Hadley, New York, in the Adirondacks, working full time as an artist.

When Bill Brown asked me to be part of this book on hand building, I did some thinking about new forms I might represent in clay. I wanted a massive form that could successfully exploit the potential strength of clay. This arch—technically a post-and-lintel structure—is over seven feet tall and as such does fulfill this potential. Traditionally, the post and lintel is a stone structure, and someday I'd like to try it that way, but our purpose here was to demonstrate that it could be achieved in clay. Large pieces *can* be made from clay; it's a very durable material and has proved itself so through the ages. It's important to keep in mind that with this arch the finished form maintains the characteristics and integrity of clay.

I can see no connection between hand building and throwing, other than the fact that they both use the same material. I do throw, but it has no place in my sculptural work (although thrown-container forms have taught me a great deal about volume). I see myself as an artist,

Figure 1. The base of the arch is first wedged out on paper. Since the arch will be built upside down, this is actually the top of the piece.

a

b

99

and the choice of technique and materials depends entirely on the idea I'm dealing with.

That's why I don't emphasize craft. The dangerous tendency of the craft world is that people make a profession out of making things fit right. To me, that's starting at the wrong end. One has to let oneself progress mentally beyond the point of technique. (I can teach the technique of hand building, for instance, in nine hours.)

When I give workshops at craft schools I try to get students to see this. Very often they can't understand why I'm not particularly interested in glazes, clay bodies, or the correct firing temperature. I'm interested in making beautiful, significant objects and in seeing, too, that they are preserved. With clay this means, of course, that the technique of firing

a

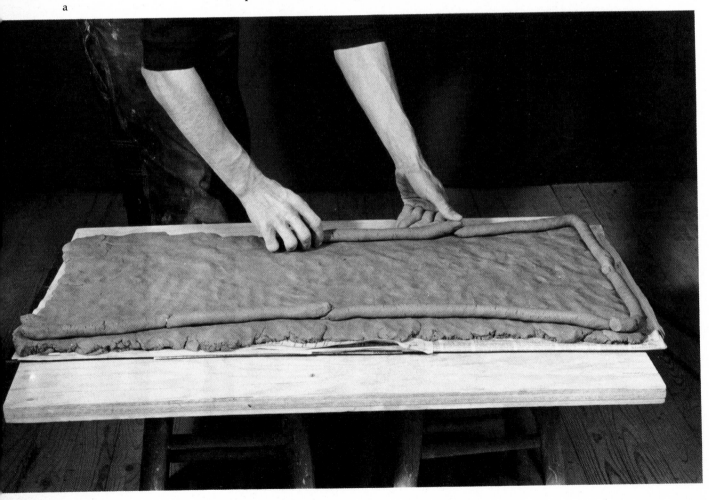

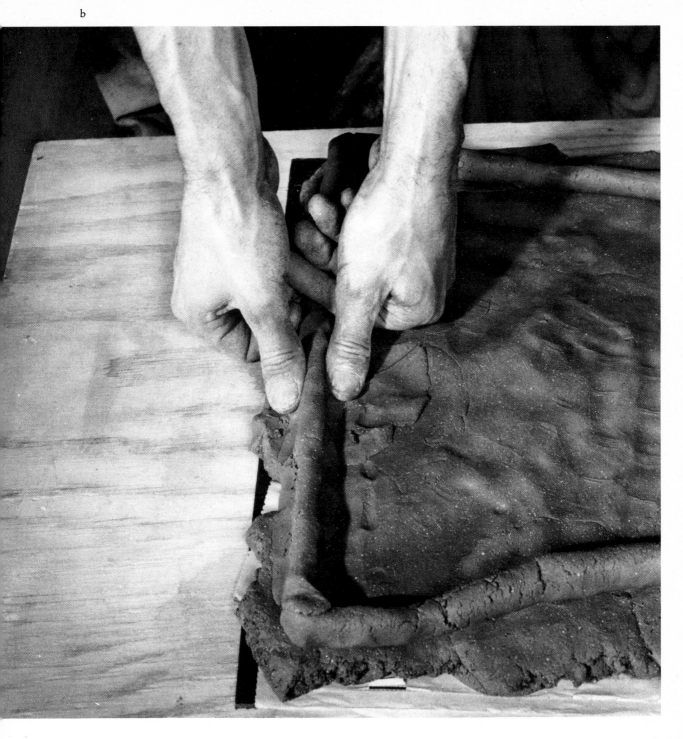

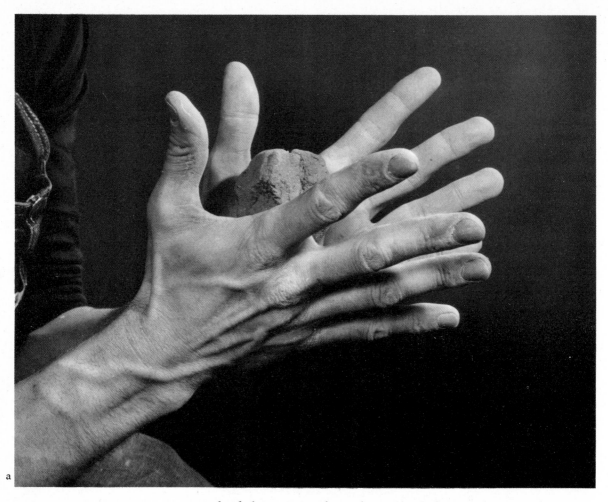

a

Figure 3. Coiling is done in the hands, moving the palms slowly, like the balance wheel of a clock.

is involved—but, again, the technique is only a tool; given the wrong circumstances it can become a trap that robs creativity. The difference between art and craft is in the individual, in his attitude. It's not a matter of saying "I'm an artist" or "I'm a craftsman." Those are fairly meaningless labels. The difference lies in the standard of values a person acquires, whether his concern with form or function takes precedence. Art does not begin where craft leaves off.

Laying the first coil of any piece is like laying the foundation of a house. (Figure 1, a and b) It's not the total design, just the basis. These coils are pinched on, and the technique is simple—no water, no slip. (Figure 2, a and b) The walls are generally about one-half inch thick.

When teaching coil construction I can see when a student has made a breakthrough in technique by the rhythm of the surface of the piece. There's a consistency to the surface that shows. My coiling, and consequently my walls, have become thinner over the years as I've tried to simplify the shapes I work with. The shapes I made six or seven years ago are much more complicated, more organic, and it's taken more control to arrive at minimal shapes. The thinness of my walls occurred naturally as I gained control over the forms.

I originally made coils by rolling them on a tabletop, but in 1963 Henry Takamoto came to my studio and showed me how to coil. My first coils made by the new method were terrible, but once I mastered it I had much greater freedom in construction. It's fairly simple—the coil is kept in

b

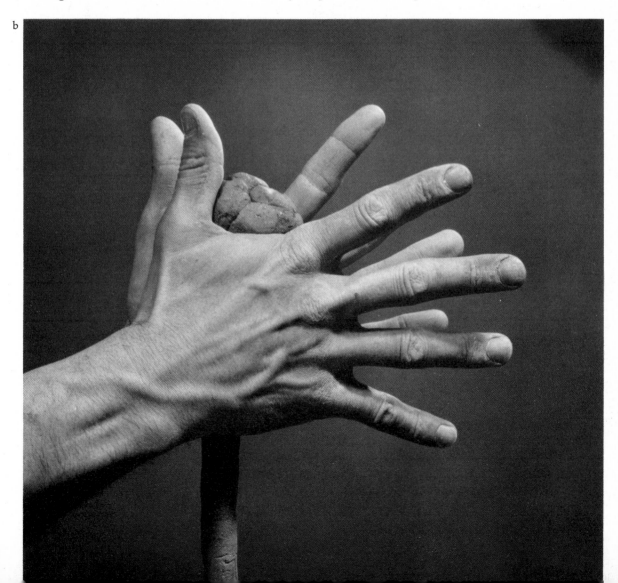

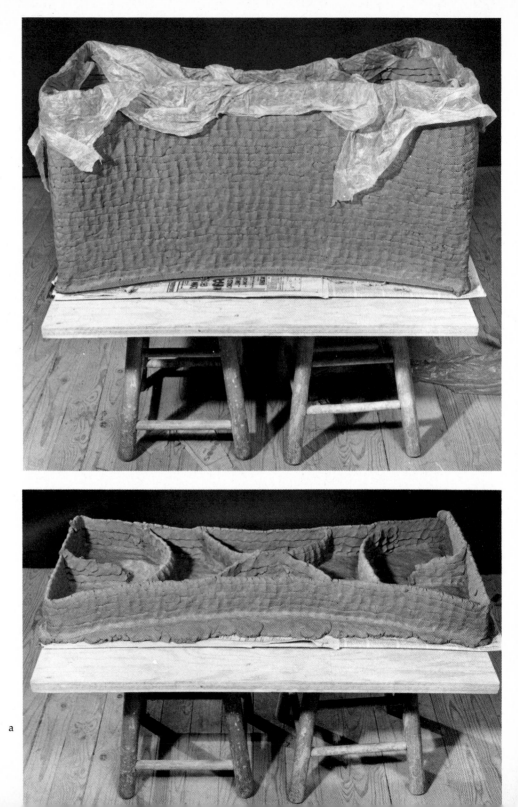

Figure 4. A thin piece of plastic around the outside and inside of the top of the wall prevents the clay from drying.

Figure 5. Curved ribs are placed on the inside of the arch to reduce stress on the walls. These ribs are built up through the entire arch.

a

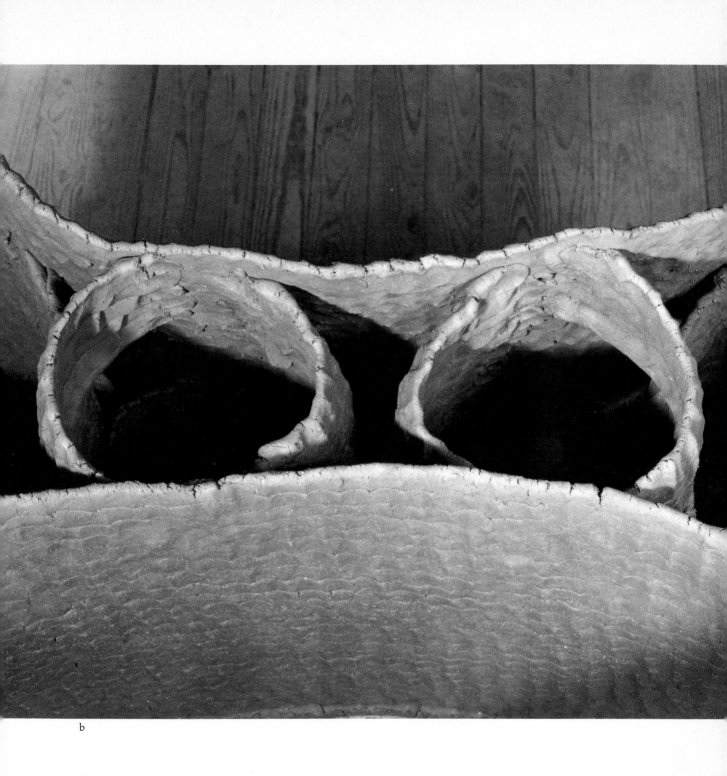

Figure 6. Cracks do occur in the coils, but the interior structure will hold the shape.

Figure 7. The lintel is closed off on top, leaving holes for the reinforcement pipes.

the palms of the hands, never touching the fingers (when rolling on table-tops the coil is always on the fingertips). The coil is turned slowly and rhythmically; it moves sort of like the balance wheel of a clock, never taking more than a quarter turn. (Figure 3, a and b).

Before starting any piece I make sketches of what I have in mind. They are a vital part of the project, though the finished product may certainly deviate to some degree. But ideas take shape in sketches. I find that I go back to old sketchbooks to pick up on ideas I've never finished, something like keeping a diary. I also sketch after work on the piece has begun, to help solve specific problems.

During my first day of work on the arch it was hard to visualize the finished object. That's the challenge with a new project. Since I had never previously attempted such a huge concave form I was a bit anxious about the outcome. Part of my problem was simply distraction—as this was to be a large-scale experiment, there were students and observers on hand all the time, not to mention the photographer who took these pictures. Once I began to build, however, I managed to sense the volume of the piece and see how the wall would take shape.

Occasionally a particular design is impossible to create right side up in clay. This design happened to fall in that category, so I worked on the piece, beginning with the lintel, upside down. I learned this technique about fifteen years ago in Minnesota when I was apprenticed to a stone carver. Mirrors can help to give an idea of the final form.

To make the three elements of the arch—the lintel and two pillars —I needed about three hundred pounds of clay. That's an enormous amount, and like any clay it had to be wedged to establish a uniform consistency. I want clay to be familiar to my touch each time I return to it.

The first slab I formed would, when finished, be the flat top of the arch. I pounded out the slab of clay over several layers of newspaper; with a very large slab, the newspaper allows the clay to shrink freely without cracking. To help avoid cracks in firing such a large piece, I added a small amount of sawdust to the mixture and about 30 percent grog.

It's obvious from the photos that there *are* cracks in my coils, due to shortness (lack of plasticity) in the clay. This would worry someone who throws, but shortness is not that crucial in coil construction. Actually, these cracks help to hold the next coil. I treat clay much as I would treat wood. Sometimes it cracks, and that's okay. This piece had so much extra stress on it—the arch is narrow in the center and heavy on the sides—that it cracked slightly in drying, but once it was fired I used epoxy to fill in the cracks.

With hand building it's generally impossible to finish a piece in one sitting, and when you come back to the work, the top three or four coils must be as soft as when you left. Then, when clay is added on, it keeps the same consistency. The bottom of the piece, though, should begin to dry so that it can hold up the higher walls; so when I leave a work I wrap a thin piece of plastic around the inside and outside of just the top of the wall to prevent the clay from drying. (Figure 4) The plastic should never cover the object completely—if it does, water will condense inside and flow to the base. Leave open space to let air reach the object.

I tried to estimate where the greatest stresses would be, and built in rib-work throughout the arch to help hold the piece together; this allowed me to do work that otherwise would have been impossible. The ribs, which have nothing to do with holding the piece up and will give little strength after the firing, were used to support the piece during the drying and firing processes. I worked with curved ribbing because it has spring to it and puts less stress on the outside walls. I placed the curved ribs inside the piece where I felt they were necessary. (Figure 5, a and b) They gave the arch the necessary internal strength, without rigidity. In doing this I followed no hard and fast rule. The only way really to judge is through experience. If the clay cracks, it cracks, but if I have enough

Figure 9. The pillars also contain ribs and are built as a pair.

interior structure, the cracks won't alter the shape; I won't lose the object. (Figure 6)

There are a lot of potters who would object to this attitude as sloppy craftsmanship. But I'm not a potter. I respect their values, but mine are not the same. I'm not afraid of my material; I feel secure in using it and I know the limits of clay. That's something that cannot be taught; it can only be learned from personal experience. These pillars, for example, conceivably could have warped during the firing. I built them to the full size of the kiln and they were placed close to the burners. But I was not so worried about possible warping that I hesitated to try for this giant size, for I was curious to see the results.

I finish off the lintel by closing off the top. While building the concave walls I worked with my thumbs inside the object, but now they

Figure 10. The surface of all pieces is scraped down after it has begun to dry.

Figure 11. White slip is brushed onto the pillars and lintel.

Figure 12. All three pieces are stacked and fired at once, but only to Cone 4.

111

are shifted to the outside as I coil up over the top, giving me greater control. (Figure 7) Where the lintel joins the pillars I will make two round holes. The pillars and lintel will be reinforced with two lengths of pipe, and the pipes secured to a heavy base when the piece is set in its permanent spot.

I next begin to work on the pillars. Again I start the base on layers of newspaper. Again, this allows the clay to shrink freely without cracking. (Figure 8) The pillars also have curved ribs within them, and are built as a pair. (Figure 9)

When the pillars and lintel are completed and have begun to dry, I smooth them down with scraping. I'm trying to define the shape by scraping the surface to a more refined state. (Figure 10) I'm not getting rid of the texture, I'm changing it, making the piece look more massive.

Painting the white slip on lintel and pillars is not just a matter of whitewashing. It's more like the feeling an artist has in preparing a canvas for a painting—a certain thrill about the potential of the piece. (Figure 11) The white lends volume and a stronger presence. I use a slip formula prepared by Cynthia Bringle, one of Penland's resident potters:

kaolin	40 parts by weight
ball clay	40 parts by weight
nepheline syenite	50 parts by weight
flint	60 parts by weight
borax	10 parts by weight
bentonite	2 percent
super pax	15 percent

I fired the piece at a lower temperature than the clay is capable of withstanding; it could have gone as high as Cone 10, but I fired only to Cone 4. Reducing the temperature won't necessarily eliminate cracking and warping, but it will cut down on it. (Figure 12)

Clay has character and prejudices. There are certain things it won't do. For example, I can't make flying objects with it, pieces with long, fragile extensions; they'll break off. Every material—wood, marble, clay—has its own capabilities, which one quickly learns. There are certain things that are possible only with clay—quick results, for one. It took me two days to make this arch; if it had been marble I would have been working for months. It is this very quality of clay that makes me feel somewhat casual, for clay doesn't demand the patient effort other materials do. Yet the challenge is always there, and I get ideas from clay that I follow up in other materials. Once I start searching, I continue.

Dish Monument. 43" high x 36" wide

Fin. 32″ high

Gold Eagle. 23″ high

Graveyard. 5' high x 21' wide x 21' deep

Six Goblets
Cynthia Bringle

Cynthia Bringle has been a resident potter at Penland School of Crafts since 1970 and is perhaps the best known of the production potters from Penland. Her functional pottery is sold throughout the United States and abroad. At Penland, North Carolina, she owns and operates her own studio and works full time as a production potter. In this chapter she describes how to throw a goblet, one of the mainstays of her production pieces.

Cynthia Bringle was born in Memphis, Tennessee. She studied at Southwestern College of Memphis and received a B.F.A. degree from Memphis Academy of Arts and an M.F.A. from Alfred University in Alfred, New York.

Among many shows, her work has appeared recently in Objects for Preparing Food at the Museum of Contemporary Crafts in New York and the Renwick Gallery, Smithsonian Institution, in Washington, D.C., 1972; Women in Porcelain at the Philadelphia Art Alliance in Philadelphia, 1973; and the Signature Shop and Gallery in Atlanta, Georgia, 1973.

Her pottery is in the collections of the Smithsonian Institution; Brooks Memorial Art Gallery in Memphis, Tennessee; Mint Museum of Art in Charlotte, North Carolina; the State of Tennessee; and the Atlanta Arts Festival in Atlanta, Georgia.

Cynthia Bringle has taught at Haystack Mountain School of Crafts in Deer Isle, Maine; Memphis Academy of Arts; Arrowmont School of Crafts in Gatlinburg, Tennessee; Naples Mill School in Naples, New York; and Penland School of Crafts. She lives in Penland, North Carolina.

Six Goblets. Stoneware, slip decoration; 9"–10" high

My interest in art goes back to the Saturday painting classes I took when I was in junior high school. There were no art classes in the high school I attended, so I had to study on my own. After high school I spent a year at a liberal arts college and then enrolled at Memphis Academy of Arts, thinking that I would major in painting.

In the first year I took a required pottery course and liked it so much that I continued it my second year. Soon I was spending most of my spare time in the pot shop. I was there when they opened the doors in the mornings, and I stayed until I was thrown out in the evenings. I also went to Maine for several summers and studied at Haystack Mountain School of Crafts.

I knew in my senior year that I wanted to set up my own studio, so after receiving my B.F.A. in 1962 I went to graduate school at Alfred University to expand my technical knowledge. When I graduated from

Figure 1. To make the stem, the top portion of the clay is centered.

Alfred in the summer of 1964, I started looking for a place to set up a studio. Eventually I rented an old house in Eads, Tennessee, and had my pottery shop set up by the spring of 1965. Then, in 1970, I decided to move to the North Carolina mountains where Penland School of Crafts is located. My involvement with Penland had begun in 1963 when I agreed to spend a few weeks working with Bill Brown. The first stoneware kiln was begun at that time. I began teaching summer sessions at Penland in 1964, and I have continued to teach there every summer since that time.

I'm a production potter because I like to make pots. I don't think a production potter is any better or any worse than anyone else who works in clay. Everyone has to decide for himself the best way to work. I like to make many different kinds of pots; as a production potter I don't produce simply one kind of mug or one casserole.

Figure 2. The clay is opened with the thumb of the right hand.

If I sit down and make a dozen casseroles they may all hold two quarts, but they will all be different. I like to make functional ware and I like to think that my pieces are being used, not collecting dust. Most of my pieces begin on the wheel. I then alter them by incising, cutting, carving, stamping, and various other techniques. I do a lot of decorating on the ware in the bisque state before glazing with slips. The time spent decorating and doing the brushwork is often longer than the original throwing of the piece.

Learning the basics of throwing is not difficult if you are willing to work, practice, and give yourself time to gain the skills. What is really important is what you do with the piece in terms of form and design. Too many people today are trying to be potters without the proper background. They take the trouble to learn only a little bit and then they start in working. Students in pottery need a background in the arts, especially in drawing and painting. Also, they need to learn to sit back and look at what they have made. We learn by studying our work, not by just producing it.

Figure 3. The clay is pulled up with both hands.

Figure 4. The stem is formed mainly by the right hand with the fingers acting as a scissors.

Figure 5. The stem is smoothed out with a rib.

Figure 6. The top of the stem is flared.

I throw all my goblets off the hump. I do the bottoms first, then the tops. When throwing off the hump of clay, all that has to be centered is the top position—the part that will be used. (Figure 1)

The clay is centered, then opened up with my thumb. (Figure 2) While I work, I keep water on the clay to lubricate it. I pull the clay open and then I start pulling up the walls. The first pullup of the wall is with the thumb and fingers of the left hand. At the same time the fingers of the right hand are also pressing in and pulling up the clay. (Figure 3) To shape the stem, I squeeze the clay between the fingers of my right hand while pressing with the left from the outside. (Figure 4)

The stem is shaped according to the type of base I want. Sometimes I use a rib to smooth it out (Figure 5), or else I finger certain parts for emphasis. The top of the stem is flared out for the base of the cup. (Figure 6) Most of my goblets are eight or nine inches tall, though I have made them as high as fourteen inches. When I have formed the stem, I cut the bottom with a wooden tool and then cut the stem off the hump with a string.

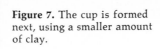
Figure 7. The cup is formed next, using a smaller amount of clay.

Figure 8. To create the design, the clay is pinched between the thumb and forefinger.

Figure 9. The cup is cut off the base by (a) tooling away the excess clay; (b) slicing through the bottom with a string; (c) lifting the cup off.

a

b

The cup is thrown next. I start the same way as with the bottom, but generally I use less clay. (Figure 7) After this particular cup is thrown, I alter the form by pressing out with a finger from the inside of the cup, then pinching the clay with the thumb and forefinger of the right hand. (Figure 8) I also pinch the clay at the top with the thumb and forefinger, to create additional design.

To take the cup off the hump, I angle in at the base of the cup with a wooden tool, which gets rid of excess clay and shapes the base (Figure 9a); then I cut the cup off with a string. (Figure 9, b and c)

Usually I work in series, making ten to twenty stems and tops

Figure 10. After the goblet is leather dry, it is sponged clean.

Figure 11. A fettling knife is used to trim the cup.

at one time. When they are leather hard—stiff but still damp—I put them together and do the decoration. It takes four to five times as long to put the goblets together and decorate them as it does to throw them.

When the pieces are leather dry, I go through and finish off each goblet, starting with the base. I use my fingers and a sponge, running them around the bottom of the base to wipe it clean. (Figure 10)

I then take the top and trim it by hand with a fettling knife. (Figure 11) I could put the goblet back on the wheel, but I prefer to work with a knife, cutting away the excess clay.

When both sections are ready, I score the bottom of the goblet

129

Figure 12. The sections are joined together by (a) scoring the top of the stem; (b) applying slip; (c) fitting the cup into place.

and the top flare of the stem (Figure 12a), put in slip (Figure 12b), and fit the pieces together (Figure 12c), letting them sit for a few minutes before wiping away the excess slurry.

Next the assembled goblet is decorated by various techniques: stamping, carving, fastening, scalloping. (Figure 13, a–c).

One of the hardest parts of being a producing potter is self-discipline. Some mornings I may not want to go down to the studio, but I do anyway. If throwing were the only thing a potter did, it would be easy. What is hard to do—but necessary—are the related jobs, everything from mixing clay to fixing equipment and handling the bookkeep-

b

c

ing, all part of what it takes to be a successful production potter.

Of course, the reason I put up with all that is because I like working with clay. I like clay because it is plastic and it has a great immediacy. I can sit at the wheel and change it any way I want. I also keep changing, making new things from clay. Most potters, I'm sure, do not have enough time in the day to do all the things they'd like to do in clay. Ceramics is not something static. Every day that I work I learn something more about what I'm doing.

After the goblet is bisque fired, three or four slips are applied before it is glazed. Most of my goblets have a combination of glazes on them. I have been making goblets for over seven years and I have yet to tire of them. For me, no two goblets are alike.

a

b

c

Figure 13. The goblet is decorated by (a) stamping; (b) carving; (c) scalloping the stem.

Two Pitchers. Stoneware; slip decoration; left, 5^1/$_2$" high x 5^1/$_2$" wide; right, 12" high x 6^1/$_2$" wide

Covered Jar. Stoneware;
slip decoration underneath;
12$\frac{1}{2}$" high x 8" wide

Covered Porcelain Jar. Slip
decoration; salt-glazed;
7$\frac{1}{2}$" high x 7" wide

Platter. Stoneware; polished and brushed glaze decoration; 14³/₄" across

Thrown Form
Toshiko Takaezu

Toshiko Takaezu is an internationally known artist who works in ceramics as well as weaving and painting. In ceramics she forms bowls, plaques, and sculpture pieces and works in both stoneware and porcelain. Her piece for this book is made by throwing and coil building, an ancient Korean technique.

Toshiko Takaezu was born in Pepeekeo, Hawaii. She was educated at the Honolulu Academy of Arts and the University of Hawaii in Honolulu, and at Cranbrook Academy of Art in Bloomfield Hills, Michigan. Among many shows, her work has appeared recently at the Contempoary Arts Center of Hawaii in Honolulu, 1966; Swarthmore College in Swarthmore, Pennsylvania, 1968; the Boise Art Association in Boise, Idaho, and Lewis and Clark College in Portland, Oregon, 1971; the Benson Gallery in Bridgehampton, New York, 1972; and the Honolulu Academy of Arts in Honolulu, 1973. Her work is in many public collections, among them the Smithsonian Institution in Washington, D.C.; the Galleries of the Cranbrook Academy of Art in Bloomfield Hills, Michigan; the Museum of Contemporary Crafts in New York; the Honolulu Academy of Arts in Honolulu; the George Peabody College Museum in Nashville, Tennessee; Detroit Institute of Art in Detroit, Michigan; the Bangkok Museum in Bangkok, Thailand; the Baltimore Museum in Baltimore, Maryland; and the Johnson Wax Collection in Racine, Wisconsin. Toshiko Takaezu has taught at Princeton University in Princeton, New Jersey; Flint Institute of Art in Flint, Michigan; Cranbrook Academy of Art; the University of Wisconsin in Madison; Cleveland Institute of Art in Cleveland, Ohio; Honolulu Academy of Arts; Haystack Mountain School of Crafts in Deer Isle, Maine; the University of Hawaii in Honolulu; and Penland School of Crafts. She lives in Clinton, New Jersey.

Thrown Form. Stoneware; 33" high

Sculpture was my first interest when I was a student many years ago in Hawaii. At that time I realized that to do sculpture one had to give oneself totally to it, and I wasn't prepared then to commit my life in such a way. I thought ceramics might be different, so I began to study clay. I was later to find out that clay was much more demanding than I had first anticipated.

From Hawaii I went to Cranbrook to study ceramics. I had already begun teaching, but I felt the need to continue to study; seeing Maija Grotell's work, which made a deep impression on me, I decided to study at Cranbrook. I took with me some volcanic black sand, which we have acres and tons of on Hawaii and which I thought was a material I should learn to use. That was in 1951, and I expected to be away from the island only one year. As it turned out, since that time I have returned to Hawaii only for one year, to teach, and to visit during the summers.

At Cranbrook several things happened to me. I began to experiment with glazes and forms and even other mediums—I studied weaving and sculpture as minor subjects—and I found that I didn't want to be limited by this one material, my volcanic black sand from Hawaii.

I had been working in many different ceramic forms, in Hawaii and at Cranbrook, and after many years a natural pure form arrived, one which I enjoy and also one on which I could paint. I didn't want a flat surface to work on, but a three-dimensional one. There was a double challenge for me here: to use color, and then to try to maintain that color at the temperatures required for stoneware firing. It took years before I was able successfully to merge the glaze as painting to the form, so that the two—painting and form—became one total and complete piece. In some ways this form and the painting on it have returned me to sculpture and painting on canvas. The form that appeals to me the most is one that suggests roundness, such as the large piece I have done here.

When I was a student at Cranbrook, I was very fortunate to have Maija Grotell as my teacher. She was an unusual and rare human being who felt it was important for students to become individuals, and it was through her criticism that I began to discover who I was. That was the beginning of my realizing that everyone has to be individualistic in their work, and that realization has played an important role in the way I teach students today. Everyone is unique and everyone should do his or her own work.

I am often asked, do I consider myself an artist, or a craftsman? To me an artist is someone quite special. You are not an artist simply

Figure 1. Sixty-five pounds of wedged clay are centered on the wheel; no bat is used.

Figure 2. The center of the clay is opened up. The heel of the right hand presses down into the clay.

Figure 3. The pot is opened up, leaving a bottom inside.

because you paint or sculpt or make pots that cannot be used. An artist is a poet in his or her own medium. And when an artist produces a good piece, that work has mystery, an unsaid quality; it contains a spirit and is alive. There's also a nebulous feeling in the piece that cannot be pinpointed in words. That to me is good work!

When working with clay I take pleasure from the process as well as from the finished piece. Every once in a while—very seldom—I am in tune with the material, and I hear music, and it's like poetry. Those are moments that make pottery truly beautiful for me.

I don't think of making pots in terms of whether they will be functional. I just make them! I like to make a plate, for example, that can be used and that when it's not in use is still complete in itself.

In 1955 I went to Japan to study the tea ceremony so that I could understand how to make tea bowls. At that time, I realized that even though I made bowls, I wasn't ready to make tea bowls. It was easy to make bowls, but to make *tea bowls* I first had to be an individual.

a

Figure 4. The walls are
pulled up with the use of
both hands.

b

Figure 5. To speed the drying process, newspaper is burned inside the base.

And at that time, I wasn't ready for tea ceremony bowls. I had to wait until making tea bowls came naturally to me. I knew in time it would happen, and it did. I knew myself well enough as a person to know when I was ready. It wasn't a question of technique; it was the question of being ready as a person.

All changes in my work come naturally—sometimes by mistake, like dropping a piece into the pot accidentally. I have learned to be patient and wait for change. When it comes, I'm ready.

In my life I see no difference between making pots, cooking, and growing vegetables. They are all related. However, there is a *need* for me to work in clay. It is so gratifying, and I get so much joy from it, and it gives me many answers for my life.

One of the best things about clay is that I can be completely free and honest with it. And clay responds to me. The clay is alive and responsive to every touch and feeling. When I make it into form, it is alive, and even when it is dry, it is still breathing! I can feel the response in my hands, and I don't have to force the clay. The whole process is an interplay between the clay and myself, and often the clay has much to say. When it is bisqued it is no longer organic, but it comes alive again in the finishing touch of the last firing—in the interplay of glaze and form.

The kiln contributes much to the piece, depending on the way it has been fired, the atmosphere, and the weather. Often it can change the whole character of the piece. Many times when I open the kiln the piece is different from what I had anticipated or planned, sometimes better and sometimes a complete surprise. To understand the kiln and to learn how to work with it is another interesting aspect of the whole process.

When I first became involved with clay, I found it had so many possibilities. To be able to carry out my ideas, to make anything good, I had to have technique and discipline. I have disciplined myself in many ways in order to achieve my ideas. What is most important is to keep on working—you can't wait for inspiration because that may never come. Inspiration most often comes when I begin to work.

Technique is very important, but it is also important to forget the technique, to have the technique inside you and out of the way. In working, the first step is the idea, the second step is the technique, and these two allow you to complete the object.

Sometimes it is better not to have technique—then you don't know the limitations of the material, and any idea becomes possible!

I have found that I have to work. The work is part of me. When I'm enjoying myself there's life in the work, and that's what's important!

145

The piece here is made by an ancient Korean technique that is a combination of throwing and coiling. This technique permits the construction of extremely large pots, much larger than one could possibly throw. The piece is begun by throwing the base. Sixty-five pounds of clay are used to make a pot over 18 inches high. The clay is centered on the wheel without the use of a wooden bat. (Figure 1)

The clay is opened by pressing down with the heel of the right hand. (Figure 2) This is very difficult work and requires constant pressure. The pot is opened up, but a bottom is left at the base. (Figure 3) This is a thick base, but before the pot is finished, the excess clay on the base will be cut away.

The walls of the piece are pulled up with both hands till a height

Figure 6. When the pot is about 18 inches high, coiling is used to enlarge the piece. This is a Korean technique that permits very large pots to be made.

a

of 18 inches is reached. (Figure 4, a–c) From this point on, the coiling technique is used. Thick coils are used, over one inch in diameter. With the pot still on the wheel, the wheel is turned slowly while the coils are worked into place with the hands. This coil building is done rapidly; to prevent the soft coils from dropping into the pot, the clay is force-dried. To speed up the drying process, newspapers are burned inside the pot. (Figure 5) A large pot like this can then be finished within four or five hours. If the forced drying was not used, it would take three days of alternately coiling and waiting for the coils to dry before the pot could be completely finished.

The coils are added—one at a time—and pinched into place (Figure 6, a and b); then the inside is smoothed as the pot is turned on the wheel.

Figure 7. The excess clay is cut away with a wooden tool to make a level surface before the next coil is added.

Figure 8. The addition of new coils changes the shape of the pot, gradually closing it in at the top.

Figure 9. The top of the piece is tapped with a wooden paddle to redefine the texture of the clay. This gives the completed piece a variety of surfaces.

The top of each coil is leveled after it is set in place. (Figure 7) This step isn't completely necessary, but it helps to produce an even surface for the addition of the next coil. As additional coils are worked into place, the shape of the pot gradually changes (Figure 8), until finally the top is closed.

While the pot is being built, small newspaper fires are started at various times in order to dry the clay. This keeps the clay from falling in on itself during the building. The total time for building the pot is about four hours. When the coiling is finished, the top section is paddled, which adds a second surface texture to the large piece. (Figure 9) A small hole is made in the top, to ensure that the piece will dry. (Figure 10)

All work on the pot is done directly on the wheel—no wooden bat is used; by working this way, the pot can be easily turned for easy access. After the object is dried to a leather-hard condition, it is removed from the wheel. It is then bisqued, decorated, and fired to its finished form.

Figure 10. An air vent is made at the top to enable the piece to dry.

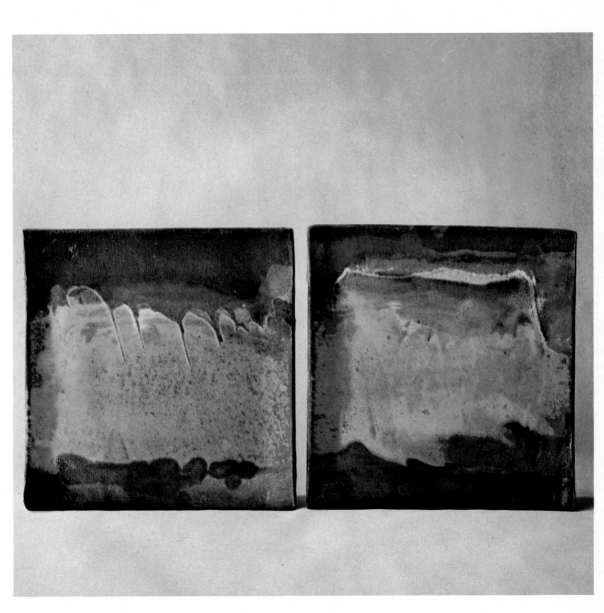

Makaha Blue. Stoneware plaques; each 12″ x 12″

Mist. Porcelain; 2″ high x 12″ across

Uariramba. Porcelain; 5³/₄″ high x 6¹/₂″ wide

Air. Porcelain; 7″ high x 8″ wide

Trio. Porcelain; all 7″ high; from the left: 5″ wide, 6″ wide, 4¹/₂″ wide

Light. Stoneware; 8¹/₂″ high x 5¹/₂″ wide

Form One
Donald Reitz

Donald Reitz is best known for the unique way he throws. For several years he has been throwing forms upside down on the wheel, a technique he demonstrates in this chapter.

Donald Reitz was born in Sunbury, Pennsylvania. He received a B.S. degree from Kutztown State College in Kutztown, Pennsylvania, and an M.F.A. in ceramics from Alfred University in Alfred, New York.

His work has appeared in many shows, among them the Smithsonian Institution in Washington, D.C., 1968; the XXIII, XXIV, and XXV International Competition of Ceramics in Faenza, Italy, 1969, 1970, 1971; Northern Arizona University in Flagstaff, 1970; Objects USA: Johnson Wax Traveling Show, 1970; National Invitational at the Museum of Contemporary Crafts in New York, 1972; Milwaukee Art Center in Milwaukee, Wisconsin, 1972; and the Victoria and Albert Museum in London, 1973.

His work is in the collections of the Smithsonian Institution; the Dave Campbell Memorial Collection in New York; the Antonio Prieto Memorial Collection at Mills College in Oakland, California; the Sybil Laubenthal Memorial Collection in Edmonton, Alberta, Canada; the Chicago Art Institute in Chicago; the Johnson Wax Collection in Racine, Wisconsin; Gilmore Art Center in Kalamazoo, Michigan; and the Gillette Permanent Collection in Sparta, Wisconsin.

Donald Reitz has taught at the University of Wisconsin in Madison and at Penland School of Crafts. He lives in Spring Green, Wisconsin.

Form One. Salt-glazed stoneware; sprayed oxide, glaze accent; 36" high

I'm a meat cutter by profession, but I've also driven trucks, cut lumber, lived with the Indians in Canada, pulled fish nets, and done a hundred other odd jobs before I got into pottery. It wasn't until I was thirty years old that I decided life was too short to spend it doing things I didn't want to do. I was newly married then and had responsibilities, but my wife agreed with me; so I quit the meat cutting business and started college to study painting.

I didn't think about clay until the last semester of my senior year, when I discovered the clay room at Kutztown State and began to throw. There has never been a time when I couldn't throw, couldn't center. Centering was a natural thing for me and I got hooked on clay immediately. I went on to Alfred University and studied ceramics for my M.F.A. Since graduating I've been a full-time potter and teacher at the University of Wisconsin.

The only reason I teach—the only reason anyone should teach—is because I like it. To teach to support your art, I think, is a very bad thing. I like teaching! I like clay, and I like art in general. I consider myself an artist who happens to be working in clay, and my forms range from utilitarian pottery objects to sculpture.

I make a lot of utilitarian forms because I like to, but the pot form, I think, must do more than serve a utilitarian purpose. If it is just to be a utensil, then a person is better off buying a commercial import, a pot made by industry, because it's cheaper and usually the clay body is better. For me, when I make a pot I deal with it as an image, and hopefully it will enhance the life of the person who uses it. It is not enough to have a pot just to serve food in—a pot is an object that exists in space. Many times I feel that function follows form. The form must meet all the utilitarian requirements, but there has to be something more, something plus.

My work has changed over the years. I began with simple pots and those pots suggested other forms. A person needs to find the scale and the clay bodies he or she likes. I like working with large pieces of clay, but there's nothing sacred about working big. There is one nice thing about it, though—if it's big and bad, it's easy to see the faults. That makes working big more of a challenge.

Many of my forms are based on classical shapes, though hopefully I'm doing them in my own way. I have never studied art history and I don't know what it would have meant to my work if I had had such a background. Perhaps it would have changed it, perhaps not.

I do think painting and drawing are important for potters. Draw-

Figure 1. Rings are formed in the cookie to act as suction cups and help hold the bat.

Figure 2. The bat is knocked into place.

Figure 3. The bat is checked to see that it is centered.

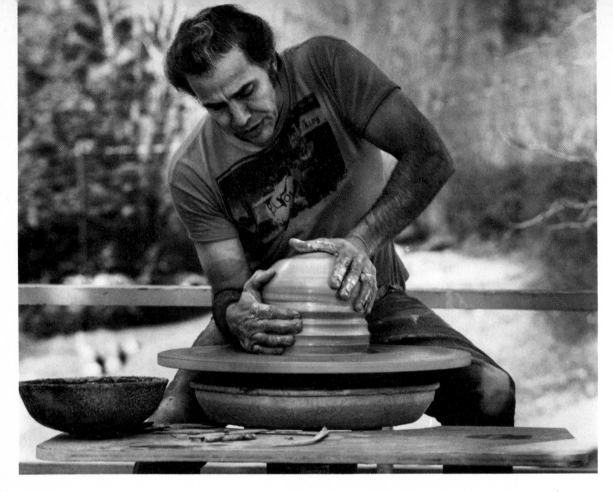

Figure 4. The clay is centered on the bat. By the inward pressure of the hands, the clay is moved up from the inside.

ing is the basis of observation—people should study drawing and painting; they help when it comes to making three-dimensional objects. A lot of pottery—a lot of sculpture—is treated as two-dimensional, even though physically it's three-dimensional; one cannot get past the surface of the object. I like to be able to get through the whole pot with my mind. I like to be able to feel the inside and the outside working together.

It seems to me as a teacher that students usually have an esthetic sense but are lacking in technical ability. So as a teacher I push them both with ideas and forms. The technique can be learned—in fact it has to be learned, so that you can work out your abstract ideas. Learning the technique only requires hard work—lots of it.

It is not difficult, for example, to learn how to throw upside down. I have been doing it for about six years. In making a large piece, I don't like to add by coiling—I'd rather throw the piece in sections, then put the sections together. What I like to do is throw lots of objects—bowls, cylinders, and so on—set them aside until the idea of "pottery"

160

Figure 5. The clay is centered with the right hand because the clay enters that hand.

form leaves my mind, and then come back and arrange them, reassemble them, cut and add. I treat the objects as sketches until I arrive at a form I like, and then I go to the wheel and make that specific form.

I began to throw the shapes on the wheel upside down because I was having trouble with the drying process. My studio is in a barn, which is quite drafty, and the rims of my pieces would be the first to dry and warp out of shape. But the rim was the part I wanted to dry last, since I was connecting the various shapes. By throwing them upside down I solved this problem.

Usually I make quite a number of pieces at one time. To begin, I establish a thick layer of clay, called a cookie, which will support all the wooden bats I'll be using. I can then just cut off the bats as I work, without having to make a new cookie each time. To make sure that the bats will stick, I make rings in the cookie which act as suction cups to help hold the bats. (Figure 1) I then clean away the excess slurry, which

Figure 6. The clay is opened up by pressing down with the right fist.

a

b

a

Figure 7. (a) A collar is established and then (b) the clay is pulled up and over.

b

Figure 8. The clay is caught at the bottom and pulled up.

Figure 9. The lip or rim is formed.

may let the bat slip off, and then I knock the bat into place. (Figure 2)

In centering, the secret is to be over the piece; then everything is related to your center. It's much easier that way. But the first thing you have to be is centered yourself. If you're not centered, you're not going to get anything centered. You center not just with your hands, but with your guts, and with your mind.

It is important that you feel right in relation to what you're doing. So you must get the clay right. Your clay has to feel comfortable to you; it's going to feel different from someone else's clay. You also have to feel right on the wheel, and it pays to get all those factors correct before beginning.

I take pains to get myself straight at the wheel, especially since I am working with large shapes; in such work I notice every little thing that might be off. I also take pains to see that the bat is correctly centered on the cookie and the wheel. (Figure 3) I am going to be throwing two shapes that I'll put together later, rim to rim, so I want them centered before I begin.

Figure 10. The opening is checked with calipers.

Figure 11. The collar section is measured to size before throwing.

Figure 12. The third section is thrown rough to establish contrast with the other sections.

When you are beginning, take a ball of clay that fits comfortably in the hand. It is best to practice with a small shape—the size of a softball works well. Don't use hot water at the beginning; use cold water. Beginning potters tend to use too much water, and hot water especially breaks down dirt. Place the ball in the center of the bat, pat it down, and you'll have it centered before you even start the wheel.

Much of centering is a downward motion. I want to attach the clay to the bat so that it doesn't go flying off. I do cone the clay.

When thinking about centering most people think about the outside surface, but what you are really trying to do is to get the inside of the clay centered. So when pushing the clay, don't think about making the outside move, think about making the inside move. By exerting pressure on the outside, the inside begins to come up. (Figure 4)

For this shape I center a low-profile hump, centering with the right hand because the clay is entering that hand as it turns on the wheel. (Figure 5) I open the hump with my fist. (Figure 6, a and b) There are about twenty-five pounds of clay on the wheel, and I open it until I think I have enough clay to pull over. When throwing, centering, and opening up, it's not so much the strength as the constant applied pressure that's important. Clay particles will move and they'll slide.

The first pull is exactly the same, whether it is a little piece of clay or a big piece. I grab the doughnut and squeeze. Then I pick it up and bring it over while I judge the thickness with my fingers. (Figure 7, a and b) I leave the bottom part thicker because I want it to support more weight. I catch the clay at the bottom and pull it up. This can't be done rapidly. And if I keep the arch moving, it won't fall in. (Figure 8)

Figure 13. The tall cone is thrown upside down.

Figure 14. The rim of the bottom is scored.

Figure 15. The second bowl is set into place.

Figure 16. The short collar is set and centered.

I cut the piece free of the bat to help it dry faster. For this I use twisted wire, which produces a corrugated surface that stops the clay from just slipping back smoothly to the bat. I then cut the bat off the cookie and throw the second piece.

I throw the second form the same way, though this piece is shallower and more difficult to throw. I have to watch to see that I don't get a lot of undulation; otherwise the form will fall in on itself.

When I have the shape I want, I make the lip (Figure 9) and then measure it with calipers. (Figure 10) I'll want to throw the third piece, the collar, to fit this top opening.

I center the third section the same way I have the other forms. I use calipers to check the approximate size. (Figure 11) I open this piece to the bat and throw it with a rough texture so that it will contrast with the two bowls. I pull it up rough and leave scars in it. (Figure 12)

The fourth piece is a tall cone shape. I throw this one upside down, and when I turn it over—or right side up—it will have a flaring top. I'm trying to create a visual interest between the horizontal axis of the bottom and the vertical axis of the collar and cone. (Figure 13)

One of the difficult aspects of throwing in sections is trying to visualize what the total form will look like when it's assembled. Often, when working, I'll sketch on the floor with a brush to see how the piece should be formed.

When I have thrown all the forms, I leave them to dry until they're leather hard, then I begin the assembling. The first bowl is turned right side up on the wheel and a collar—a band of clay—is added to hold the piece in place. Then I score the rim to join the two bowls together. (Figure 14)

The second bowl is set down on top of the first bowl or base. (Figure 15) The rims have to be tightly sealed, both inside and out, to ensure that they don't break apart during the firing. I push the clay down from the top section as the piece turns on the wheel, and then go back again and pull up the clay from the bottom. Both the inside and the outside are sealed this way.

The third piece, the short collar, is placed on the bowls. (Figure 16) Each section is centered—they are not just put together rim to rim. Centering each section at the top ensures that the object will be straight on the wheel. This piece, too, is sealed on both sides.

The final section, the tall cone, is put on the top and fastened. (Figure 17) I want each piece to retain its own identity, though together they must add up to a unity. I can see that the collar section is not dis-

Figure 17. The tall cone is sealed on the inside.

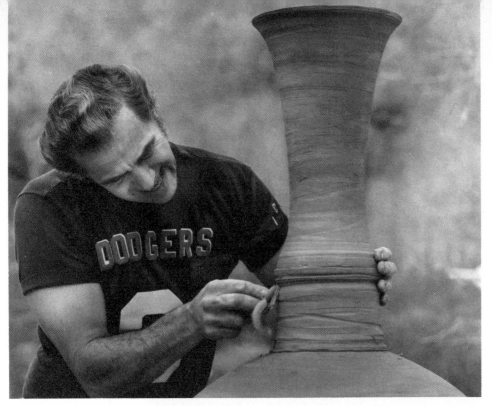

Figure 18. The collar section is sculptured with a tool.

Figure 19. An extra rim of clay is added to the cone to create a feeling of containment.

171

Figure 20. Two appendages are attached to the cone to break up the flow of space.

tinct enough and I return to it and try to loosen it up visually. (Figure 18)

The nice thing about clay is that one can remove from, add to, throw, cut into, build, and so on with the piece. What I don't like is to have the technique become overpowering. I don't like to look at an object and see that the most important thing about it is the process by which it was made.

At the top of the flared cone I add an extra ring of clay. (Figure 19) I want the feeling of containment, of volume inside the form, but the way the cylinder flares out gives the impression of the volume escaping. Therefore, I close the flare slightly.

On the cone section I attach two appendages. (Figure 20) I don't find this space on the cylinder very exciting. It's like the handle for a pitcher. It's what the handle does as it reacts to the space around it that's important. These appendages will break the flow of the piece; they will make the viewer stop a while and explore what is happening with the piece at this point. How these pieces are joined is important because the joints are part of the piece and must be dealt with in a visual manner.

With the addition of the two appendages the form is ready for firing and glazing.

Form Two. Salt-glazed stoneware; sprayed oxides, glaze, frit, feldspar accent; 24″ high

Form Four. Salt-glazed
stoneware; sprayed oxides,
glaze accent; 30" high

Form Five. Salt-glazed
stoneware; dry-rubbed and
sprayed oxides, glaze accent;
28" high

Form Three. Salt-glazed
stoneware; dry-rubbed
oxides, frit stain, glaze
accent; 18" high

Mirror Frame with Lamp
Ron Propst

Ron Propst is a production potter who has made his living from pottery since 1967. He has worked in all aspects of ceramics. For this section he has built a wall-hanging mirror frame, using both throwing and hand-building techniques.

Ron Propst was born in Hickory, North Carolina. He was educated at East Carolina College in Greenville and studied pottery at Penland School of Crafts.

His work has appeared in the Crafts U.S.A. Traveling Show, 1966; Appalachian Corridors in Charleston, West Virginia, 1967; and the Mint Museum Show in Charlotte, North Carolina,

1967. He has also had solo exhibitions at the American Crafts in Cleveland, Ohio, the Ridgeway Gallery in Oak Ridge, Tennessee, and the Piedmont Craft Shop in Winston-Salem, North Carolina, 1972; and Storehouse, Inc., in Atlanta, Houston, and Dallas, 1974.

His work is in the collections of R. Phillip Hanes, Jane and Mark Peiser, Cynthia Bringle, Dr. and Mrs. R. Leves McCarthy, and Don and Lisa Drumm.

Ron Propst has taught at Vaten School of Crafts in Bristol, Virginia, Hickory School in Hickory, North Carolina, and Penland School of Crafts. He lives in Penland, North Carolina.

Mirror Frame with Lamp. 3' high x 2' wide

Pottery and crafts in general were not important to me when I was growing up in Hickory, North Carolina. I didn't get interested in art until I went to play football at East Carolina College. College football wasn't the fun game it had been for me in high school. It was all business; and studying came second. I wasn't long at school before I realized I didn't want to play ball under those conditions.

In my first semester at college I was a history major—football players were either history or physical education majors at East Carolina —but I wasn't interested in what I was studying. Then by chance, in my biology class, a young woman who sat across from me, who was an art major, suggested that I see about a transfer to the art department.

I went to see Dr. Gray, the head of the art department at the college. He worked out a new class schedule for me and I transferred my major, first to art education and later to a B.F.A. program with a major in ceramics and a minor in sculpture. Because I had lost credits in my first year with these curriculum changes, I stayed at school during the summer and took art classes, including ceramics. That was my first pottery experience and I fell in love with clay!

The art program at East Carolina was very rigid and that was helpful. It forced me to do projects I wouldn't ordinarily do. In making

Figure 1. The clay is first flattened into a low profile on the wheel.

a career out of ceramics, I feel very fortunate to have had that broad and solid background.

I first came to Penland in 1963, just for the summer session, on a small scholarship I had won from the East Carolina College ceramics department. Every year the department holds a pottery show and raises money, which it awards to a student to go off and study somewhere else. Students from East Carolina had gone all over.

I had heard about Penland from an instructor and visited the school during the spring break. I saw the list of instructors and realized it would be impossible for me to receive the same kind of serious instruction anywhere else in the United States. After that first summer session I went back for the next five summers. And I always went early, to help Bill Brown in any way, from cutting grass to building pottery wheels.

When I left college I took a job for one year as art coordinator of the Pitt County School in Greenville, North Carolina. I didn't like that type of work. What I wanted was to be a full-time production potter. So I telephoned Bill Brown and said I was coming back to Penland in the fall and did he have a place for me? He told me to come along and that the school would work something out.

Living and working at Penland as a resident craftsman gave me

Figure 2. (a) The center is opened and (b) cut completely through to the bat.

a

b

Figure 3. The center of the inner tube is opened up.

Figure 4. *Top right:* The outside wall is pulled out to form the bottom.

Figure 5. The inside wall is established first to give room later for maneuvering.

Figure 6. Pressure is applied to both walls. This turns them in.

a

b

Figure 7. The walls are pushed over and sealed with slurry.

a

b

c

the chance to become a production potter. A college education in crafts doesn't give you what you need to know to become a production potter, to make a living from ceramics. Penland gave me time to build up my skills. It also gave me a total environment that believed in and was committed to crafts; that's very important to a beginning potter.

Another great influence on me in those early days was Byron Temple, whom I first met at Penland. In 1967 there weren't many production people making mugs, and Byron said to me, "You can make a living making mugs." And he was right. That first year I did nothing but make mugs. I must have made close to five thousand and I sold them for a dollar each wholesale. That's what I lived on during the time I was experimenting with other forms, glazes, and clays.

I've always wanted to be a production potter, to make my full

Figure 8. A rib is used to shape the top.

Figure 9. Additional pieces are thrown off the hump to be used as decoration.

a

b

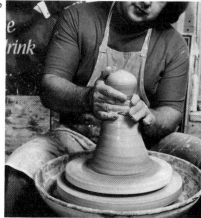

Figure 10. The additional pieces are cut off the hump with wire.

living that way. I don't think there's any basic difference between a production person and a craftsman making one-of-a-kind pieces. A production person to me is someone who reproduces a certain object that he's designed and made more than once. Now everyone does that! Toshiko Takaezu has made her bottle form continually. There has been a change in them, a progression, but a very slow progression.

I've made mugs since I first started in pottery, but the mugs I make today aren't anything like those I first did. I'm very interested in a slow progression in one direction. Production potters keep reproducing and making those productions better. If I make a piece often enough I begin to realize what is bad about it. I find that I never make my best pot the first time. On the contrary—the last one is often the best, because I've had time to look at the pot, think about it, and resolve

183

Figure 12. An edge is
established on the inside
rim for holding the mirror.

what I like and don't like about it. One-of-a-kind objects are great, but
most of the one-of-a-kind people are still taking the same form and
revising it in a certain direction. They are just as much production potters as I am!

My work has changed in many ways since I left school. I do
bigger pieces and more sculptured pieces today. I also do more decoration
on my pieces. One of the first kinds of pottery I did was flameware. Not
many people in 1967 were making pots out of flameware and I realized
I could make a living from it. I started to develop a flameware clay body
of my own at Penland. It took a whole year of experimentation. I wanted
the clay body so that it could be used in cooking; I didn't want to start
receiving letters from people saying that my flameware had cracked.

My first experiments were with a mineral called petalite. This

Figure 11. A slab is rolled
out on the machine.

Figure 13. Lines define
where the glaze will be used.

mineral is only found in Rhodesia, and just about the time I had per-
fected the clay body, the United States broke off relations with Rhodesia.
So I had to start all over and spend another year developing another
flameware clay, this time using the mineral spodumene, which is available here in the United States.

I still make flameware pottery, but lately I've gotten into some
new forms. This is because I've also become interested in plants and
planters, and as a result, my forms have become more plantlike. The
piece I am now making is a new form, using a combination of techniques—throwing and slab work; it's a mirror frame, lamp, and wall
hanging all in one.

The frame is begun by flattening out twelve pounds of clay on
a bat. (Figure 1) I flatten the clay out—instead of working from a mound—
in order to make a low-profile inner tube. Once I have set the clay, I
open the center and go all the way through, not leaving a bottom. This
leaves a doughnut shape at the edge of the bat. (Figure 2, a and b)

I open the center of the doughnut and form the walls on each
side. To open the center, I work just as I would in making a pot, pressing my fingers down, but not boring through the back side. (Figure 3)
I pull the outside wall out to form the bottom rather than pulling the
inside wall. If I were to pull inward all the time it would limit the size
of the mirror. (Figure 4)

When establishing the walls, I begin on the inside, pulling that

185

Figure 14. The pieces are collected before assembling.

Figure 15. The first section of slab is joined to the inner tube and sealed with slurry and a coil of clay.

Figure 16. A hole for the tubing that supports the lamp is cut out before firing.

up first. If I started on the outside wall, I'd obstruct my ability to get inside to the interior wall. (Figure 5) As the walls are pulled up, I begin to bow them, pushing them so they will form the tube. Slight pressure on the inside of each tube wall will push them out.

To seal the tube I begin by applying pressure on the top of the walls, starting again with the inside wall. (Figure 6, a and b) When the inside wall is pushed as far as possible, I turn the outside wall over. (Figure 7, a–c) The slip, or slurry of clay, binds the two walls together where they touch. (Figure 7d) I have never had an inner tube crack at this point; the seal holds very well. Next I take a rib and work it over the top to seal and shape the top. (Figure 8)

Now I center a smaller piece of clay once more on the wheel, to make the elements that will form the other parts of the piece. I make a variety of shapes—sometimes as many as six—and select from among them. (Figure 9, a and b) I cut them off the hump with a piece of wire. (Figure 10) These pieces will fit onto the frame to serve as decoration. I also throw another, smaller inner tube, which will be the connection for the lamp. It is tooled completely round.

The slab that joins all these pieces together is made on a machine. With my slab machine I can make a slab two feet wide and five feet long. That is more than I'll need and also it is not in the shape I want, but by cutting and shaping the slab, I can achieve the results I want. The slab machine is useful because it applies a great deal of pressure to the clay, much more than I could get by rolling, though it is possible to form the slab with a rolling pin. (Figure 11)

When the large inner tube is leather hard—dry enough to be stiff but damp enough to be joined together with slurry—I place it back on the wheel and make an edge on the inside rim where the mirror will sit. Then I flatten that area out with a wooden tool. (Figure 12) This is the area that I'll eventually glaze—so that when looking at the mirror, one will immediately see the reflection of the glaze. I mark lines where I want the glaze to go. (Figure 13) Finally, I set the tube with the other pieces and begin the arrangement. (Figure 14)

I first place the two pieces of the lamp holder—the bowl and the tube—together and seal them. Then I assemble the entire frame. I begin by cutting a piece of slab to shape; I join this to the tube by applying slurry, then adding a coil of clay. (Figure 15) This forms the back of the piece and acts as a buffer during firing—otherwise the form would crack.

I next cut out and shape slabs of clay to arrange at the top of the tube, continually adding and removing pieces of clay until I have the form I want. With a knife I mark crisscrosses on the slab, apply slurry, then paddle it into position. For additional decoration, I add one of the small forms I threw earlier on the wheel, scoring it on the back and adding slip in order to attach it to the large slab.

Before the piece is fired, while it is still in separate sections, portions of the large tube, the slab, and the other decorative parts are glazed. This is done after bisquing—the first firing—which dries the piece and leaves it porous, able to absorb water and hence the glaze. I also rub the unglazed areas with a clear stain (black glaze mixed with iron oxide and a lot of water) to preserve the natural clay surface.

For the final firing, I do not fire the whole form as one piece, because its weight would cause it to crack. I simply cut a hole in the slab for the tubing and lamp (Figure 16) and fire them separately. Later the lamp and the additional decorative form will be epoxied to the completed mirror frame.

Bird Feeder. 18″ high x 12″ wide

Wall Vase with Flowers. 9″
high x 18″ wide x 5″ deep

190